20.00

BV

SO-ATF-690

2009

"Plueddemann paints powerful pictures of how our 'low context' images of leadership blind us to the expectations and practices of people living and leading in 'high context' environments. He then guides the reader to think and reflect on how biblical principles both challenge and affirm our respective values. Following the same practice, he critiques the contemporary literature on 'power distance' and 'individualism/collectivism.' This is an important theological reflection on contemporary leadership theory (GLOBE) and its relevance for crosscultural Christian ministry."

**Sherwood Lingenfelter,** provost and senior vice president, Fuller Theological Seminary, and author of *Leading Cross-Culturally* and *Ministering Cross-Culturally*

"This book carefully integrates theory and reality in contemporary global Christian leadership. It is an invaluable tool in the hands of a leader who desires to impact our multicultural world globally and contextually. It equips, inspires, challenges and enlarges the leader's vision to a higher plane of impacting others. It frees the leader from a monocultural grid to a contemporary multicultural grid. The book integrates helpful ideas of the past with the present and brings our future world reality closer to the present on solid theological grounding."

**Dr. David K. Ngaruiya,** acting vice chancellor and head of the intercultural studies department, Nairobi International School of Theology

"*Leading Across Cultures* is one of the most informative books that I have read on the subject of crosscultural leadership. It integrates sociological data with praxis, experience with theory and, finally, actual life stories with optimal patterns of what crosscultural leadership would look like in given contexts. It is must-reading for those who intend to seriously engage in leadership in the globalized mission/church context of the twenty-first century."

**David Tai-Woong Lee,** director, Global Leadership Focus, Korea

"For years Jim's example and principles have guided me in my leading and teaching in Africa. I have tasted first-fruits of the great joy and fruitfulness I see in his life. Now in this engaging book, Jim shares his practical insights from forty years of leadership experiences and research with you. He has led influential Nigerian, American and international organizations; personally mentored leaders in fifty countries; and integrated research from business, anthropology, education and intercultural studies. Read well and lead well!"

**Rev. Steven Rasmussen,** Ph.D., founding director, Training East African Ministers, and lecturer, Nairobi Evangelical Graduate School of Theology

"I read and reread Plueddemann's book *Leading Across Cultures* with extreme excitement. I can say this book has transformed my thinking and understanding on intercultural leadership of global missions. I am thankful for his contribution and efforts not only for readers from the West but also for the global church and overall global missionary endeavor. Therefore, I hope this book will transform the understanding of many, many mission leaders, pastors and missionary trainers. It will also bring new ways of doing missions for those who are ready to change and truly want to expand God's kingdom in missions and church planting in different cultures. Reading this book with conviction will bring humility and harmony among missionary teams, inspire for action, and give direction and vision for new ways of doing missions in crosscultural contexts."

**Dr. Desta Langena,** director, Kale Heywet School of Missions, Ethiopia

"I found this an extremely helpful book and one that was screaming to be written. The results of gleaning leadership principles from different cultures and applying them can enhance a person's leadership effectiveness because the world has changed and there are few, if any, purely monocultural situations. This book is a must-read for anyone who wants to influence others in crosscultural and multicultural situations. As a dean, I would recommend it to all those who teach in higher education because of the diverse students we have in our classrooms."

**Junias Venugopal,** dean, Seminary & School of Missions,
Columbia International University

"Professor Jim Plueddemann has succeeded in achieving a rare feat. He has written a book that is scholarly and practical, biblical and contextual. Professor Plueddemann draws from his long and rich experience of leadership in Christian ministry and scholarship both in the West and crossculturally. He offers illustrations from every continent. He provides clear boundaries with his definition of *missionary* and *leadership*. One of the great strengths of this book is the assumption that all leaders from all cultures can learn from one another. No culture is perfect. As God's children endowed with the Holy Spirit, we can certainly benefit from each others' experience and walk with God. I highly recommend this book to any leader who is involved in crosscultural ministry. That is every leader because of the global context in which we live."

**Bulus Y. Galadima,** provost and associate professor,
Jos ECWA Theological Seminary, Nigeria

# LEADING

# ACROSS

# CULTURES

EFFECTIVE MINISTRY AND MISSION

IN THE GLOBAL CHURCH

## JAMES E. PLUEDDEMANN

Colo. Christian Univ. Library
8787 W. Alameda Ave.
Lakewood, CO 80226

IVP Academic
An imprint of InterVarsity Press
Downers Grove, Illinois

InterVarsity Press
P.O. Box 1400, Downers Grove, IL 60515-1426
World Wide Web: www.ivpress.com
E-mail: email@ivpress.com

©2009 by James E. Plueddemann

All rights reserved. No part of this book may be reproduced in any form without written permission from
InterVarsity Press.

InterVarsity Press® is the book-publishing division of InterVarsity Christian Fellowship/USA®, a movement of
students and faculty active on campus at hundreds of universities, colleges and schools of nursing in the United States
of America, and a member movement of the International Fellowship of Evangelical Students. For information
about local and regional activities, write Public Relations Dept., InterVarsity Christian Fellowship/USA, 6400
Schroeder Rd., P.O. Box 7895, Madison, WI 53707-7895, or visit the IVCF website at <www.intervarsity.org>.

All Scripture quotations, unless otherwise indicated, are taken from the Holy Bible, Today's New International
Version™ Copyright © 2001 by International Bible Society. All rights reserved.

While all of the stories in this book are true, some names and identifying details have been changed to protect the
privacy of those involved. Sidebar reflections are used with permission.

Design: Cindy Kiple

Images: Jim Frazier/Getty Images

ISBN 978-0-8308-2578-3

Printed in the United States of America ∞

InterVarsity Press is committed to protecting the environment and to the responsible use of natural
resources. As a member of Green Press Initiative we use recycled paper whenever possible. To learn
more about the Green Press Initiative, visit <www.greenpressinitiative.org>.

Library of Congress Cataloging-in-Publication Data

Plueddemann, Jim.
  Leading across cultures: effective ministry and mission in the
global church/James E. Plueddemann.
    p. cm.
  Includes bibliographical references and index.
  ISBN 978-0-8308-2578-3 (pbk.: alk. paper)
  1. Christian leadership. 2. Multiculturalism—Religious
aspects—Christianity. I. Title.
  BV652.1.P58 2009
  253—dc22
                          2009026589

P   20   19   18   17   16   15   14   13   12   11   10   9   8   7   6   5   4   3   2   1
Y   25   24   23   22   21   20   19   18   17   16   15   14   13   12   11   10   09

DEDICATED TO THE MEMORY OF
REV. DR. BYANG KATO
(1936-1975)

My friend and leadership mentor . . .

His dream for evangelical leadership development continues to influence millions.

His vision included Bangui Evangelical School of Theology, the Nairobi Evangelical Graduate School of Theology, and the Accrediting Council for Theological Education in Africa.

He led through vision and by example as General Secretary of the Evangelical Churches of West Africa and the Association of Evangelicals of Africa.

His heart-cry was that "African Christians be Christian Africans" and that leadership be culturally African while holding to the ever-abiding message of Scripture.

Byang Kato was a godly visionary who left a legacy of leaders for the worldwide church.

# CONTENTS

# ACKNOWLEDGMENTS

IT TAKES A COMMUNITY TO WRITE A BOOK. Trinity Evangelical Divinity School provided the opportunity to write by generously granting a sabbatical. Thank you, Dean Tite Tiénou and the Board of Regents. I'm grateful for the TEDS doctoral students who have enriched and broadened my ideas about crosscultural leadership.

Joel Scandrett of InterVarsity Press listened to my early ideas and encouraged me to submit a book proposal. Al Hsu has continued to give encouragement along with helpful insights to improve the book.

I am especially grateful for colleagues who took the time to carefully read the manuscript and graciously critique the book while making valuable suggestions: Howard Brant, Greg Campbell, Charlie Davis, Duane Elmer, Dave Horsey and Craig Ott.

Thanks to David Malone and the Billy Graham Center of Wheaton College for giving me a place to write, kindly allowing me to use an office in the library.

Our daughter Shari and son Danny, born in Nigeria, cheered me on in writing this book. As "third-culture kids" they continually enrich my life with their dedication to multicultural goals and relationships.

My talented daughter-in-law Tabitha challenged me delightfully. Her comments included, "Papi, this is the most boring sentence I've ever read," and "You are the world's expert in the use of the verb 'to be.'" She would then proceed to suggest three or four dazzling alternatives. If you read any brilliant sentences in the book, they were probably edited by Tabitha.

The book would not have been possible without Carol, my wife and beloved fellow pilgrim. I'm thankful for her editing ability and I'm grateful that our lives have been interwoven at each step of the journey.

When I was twenty-five years old I thought I knew a lot about leadership. I'm glad I didn't write this book then. Over the years, the Lord has provided rich experiences, wise counselors and opportunities to study and teach theories of leadership. I will mention many significant mentors later in the book.

# INTRODUCTION

WE LIVE IN THE MOST EXHILARATING ERA of world missions since Acts chapter 2. The worldwide body of Christ is growing rapidly, spreading widely and interacting more than ever before. Missionaries are going from everywhere and serving everywhere. But the globalization of the church also presents dangerous possibilities for crosscultural tensions, especially regarding leadership values. Church leaders must learn to cooperate with people who have radically different assumptions about leadership. From a human perspective, the hope for the worldwide church depends on effective multicultural leadership.

Today's generation of leaders in the global church must learn new skills and be willing to discard some of the styles that made them so effective in monocultural leadership. Learning to lead in the multicultural context will be disconcerting. Geert Hofstede, a pioneer in leadership and culture, writes:

> Learning to become an effective leader is like learning to play music: Besides talent, it demands persistence and the opportunity to practice. Effective monocultural leaders have learned to play one instrument; they often have proven themselves by a strong drive and quick and firm opinions. Leading in a multicultural and diverse environment is like playing several instruments. It partly calls for different attitudes and skills, restraint in passing judgment and the ability to recognize that familiar tunes may have to be played differently. The very qualities that make someone an effective monocultural leader may make her or him less qualified for a multicultural environment.[1]

*The challenge:* Christians from every nation are interacting with each other and cross-pollinating the worldwide church. Yet increased cooperation has potential for fresh tensions within the body. High on the list of misunderstandings is a clash of culturally diverse leadership values and styles. As we understand the cultural underpinnings that influence our views of leadership we will be able to work together with mutual respect.

*My hopes for the book:* I pray that the ideas presented here will be used of the Lord to foster mutual understanding, cooperation and enhanced ministry as leaders from around the world work together more effectively. Through eyes of faith, I picture multicultural teams partnering with beautiful harmony so that the body of Christ grows and is strengthened in every way. The stakes are high! I pray that believers from around the world will work together with such love and understanding that all people groups will be radically changed by the power of the gospel.

*The plan of the book:* I write from the perspective of twenty-four years of crosscultural leadership experience. Those years include mistakes, for sure. I also write from the perspective of a social scientist and academician who is committed to the full authority of the Bible. This book will seek to integrate biblical principles of leadership with social science research and experience to the end that the practice of leadership is enhanced and the worldwide body of Christ is strengthened.

## INTENDED READERS

As I interact with crosscultural practitioners, I find that virtually all have faced frustrations stemming from leadership misunderstandings. I picture the following people who could profit from the book:

- missionaries from anywhere in the world serving short-term or long-term in any other culture
- students and professors interested in leadership and culture
- mission pastors seeking to implement crosscultural, church-to-church partnerships
- church missions committees that equip, select and support the missionary force
- youth pastors and others who face the challenge of leading crosscultural short-term mission trips
- pastors of multiethnic churches

- executives of mission agencies who partner with leaders in other cultures
- pastors and parachurch ministers who receive missionaries from another culture
- crosscultural business people working under the leadership of those from a different culture
- theological educators involved in crosscultural leadership development
- crosscultural relief and development workers serving with local leadership
- mission mobilizers from scores of sending countries who seek to challenge believers with God's command to make disciples in the whole world.

## DEFINITION OF MISSIONARY

The word *missionary* has mixed connotations. For some people, missionaries are heroes and spiritual giants, worthy to be put on a pedestal. At the other extreme, missionaries are thought to be religious fanatics who destroy cultures and stir up sectarian strife. Many times, they are stereotyped as being from the West and having white skin. More recently the idea has surfaced that all believers are missionaries. I remember a missions conference with the theme, "You are either a missionary or a mission field." I recently visited a church that featured a large sign over the exit: "You are now entering the mission field." Some Christian organizations define a missionary as anyone needing to raise support. A prayer letter from a Christian camp announced that all the camp staff were missionaries, meaning the camp didn't pay them a salary. One of my American friends jokingly defines a missionary as anyone who receives a tax-deductible receipt for the cost of their travel.

Most missionaries are neither spiritual giants nor destroyers of culture. They go out from every country in the world, they have a unique calling, and they are not defined by whether they raise support or not.

*A missionary is anyone, from any country, who leaves home in order to proclaim the gospel, usually in another culture.*[2] The term is derived from the concept of "apostle," or "sent one," so by definition, missionaries move beyond their home ministries.

In the Old Testament, priests had local responsibility for taking care of the temple, while prophets spoke the word of God both to Israel and to the nations. Jesus' disciples were also called apostles or "sent ones." They were called to *leave home*, family and occupations for the sake of Jesus and for the gospel (Mk 10:29). New Testament pastors, elders and deacons were responsible for local house churches, while "apostolic bands" left home to preach the gospel. During much of the history of the church, parish priests led local congregations while religious orders[3] carried the gospel to distant places. Put simply, missionaries are people who leave home for the sake of the gospel.[4] While differences between local and nonlocal ministries become fuzzy at times, the basic distinction helps to avoid confusion of roles.[5]

Christians living or doing business in another country are not necessarily missionaries unless they intentionally seek opportunities to share the gospel.[6] Yet, communicating the gospel is not the only thing that missionaries do. They do in fact hold verbal proclamation of the gospel together with meeting human need. Through the centuries missionaries have holistically proclaimed Christ as they healed the sick, built schools, provided clean water, initiated agricultural innovation and spoke out against injustice.

When an Indian family moves away from their own culture in south India to the Islamic North in order to do the work of evangelism and discipleship, they are missionaries. Chinese family members setting up a market stall in Afghanistan for the sake of taking the gospel westward are missionaries. An Australian English teacher in China who looks for informal opportunities to share the gospel is a missionary.

### DEFINITION OF LEADERSHIP

There must be hundreds of definitions of leadership, each one reflecting philosophical, theological and cultural values. People from a goal-oriented culture might define leadership as accomplishing the task through other people. Leaders from a relationship-oriented society would prefer to define leadership as the ability to build alliances and friendships. Societies with a low tolerance for ambiguity insist on a precise definition, while those with a high tolerance for ambiguity would likely not bother with any definition.

Recently the *U.S. News & World Report* editors selected their choice of the best leaders. They defined a leader as a person who "motivates people to work collaboratively to accomplish great things."[7] The selection committee used three criteria for the best leaders: (1) they set direction; (2) by "building a shared sense of purpose," they achieved results that had a positive social impact that exceeded expectations; and (3) they cultivated a culture of growth by inspiring others to lead.[8]

Since there is no divinely inspired definition of leadership, I will show my theological and cultural bias with the following description: *Good leaders are fervent disciples of Jesus Christ, gifted by the Holy Spirit, with a passion to bring glory to God. They use their gift of leadership by taking initiative to focus, harmonize and enhance the gifts of others for the sake of developing people and cultivating the kingdom of God.*

My prayer is that God will use this book to fan into flame the leadership gifts of people in every land for the delightful and challenging task of multicultural leadership.

# PART I

# MULTICULTURAL LEADERSHIP
# IN THE WORLDWIDE CHURCH

PART ONE CALLS FOR A FRESH LOOK at the influence of culture on the theory and practice of leadership in a globalized church. If the worldwide body of Christ is to work together in harmony, a crosscultural understanding and appreciation of leadership differences is essential.

# LEADERSHIP FOR A NEW DAY
# IN WORLD MISSIONS

*Christian mission in the twenty-first century has become
the responsibility of a global church.*

SAMUEL ESCOBAR

I WAS A BIT RETICENT ABOUT CONDUCTING official business in my supervisor's living room so late in the evening, long after office hours. As I waited, a rerun of *Hawaii Five-O* blared on the television in the corner, and the room was packed with more than a dozen pastors all waiting their turn to consult with my Nigerian boss.

As the director of theological education for this large West African denomination, I was responsible for the administration of twenty-one Bible colleges and seminaries. I often needed to consult with my boss about major decisions, so I made regular appointments through his secretary. Seldom did we meet during the scheduled time. Most often he would be away on an emergency trip, or an important pastor or village chief would show up at the last minute and usurp my time slot.

On this night I was frantic. I needed a decision from my boss for a crucial board meeting. My flight left very early the next morning. One of the Bible colleges had run out of money halfway through the last semester, and the board was recommending that we close the school and send the students home! I needed to tell my boss this news and get his advice. After missing another appointment he simply told me to come to his house that evening. Even though I felt it would be rude for me to interrupt his personal and family time with my official business, I went. As I entered his living room, I noticed every chair was filled with pastors coming to him for advice or decisions. I waited my turn, somewhat embarrassed to overhear what seemed to be confidential conversations about various church discipline problems, but no one else seemed uncomfortable. At that moment I sat there feeling frustrated, impatient and confused about Nigerian leadership style.

## THE CHALLENGE

The good news is that the body of Christ has been planted and is growing in every country of the world to the extent that churches in the non-Western world are now the majority. The globalization of the church and the general accessibility of cheap air travel have led to unprecedented international interconnectedness.

- Millions of short-termers travel from scores of countries every year to just about every country of the world.
- Tens of thousands of long-term missionaries from Africa, Asia and Latin America now serve in every country of the world.
- Christian colleges and universities are becoming intentionally globalized.
- Urban centers worldwide are forging new multicultural ministries.
- Global business people often see their work as ministry.
- A high percentage of missionaries are working under the leadership of national church leaders.
- Hundreds of churches are forming mission partnerships with other churches around the world.
- Whole denominations in the West are coming under the direction of African leaders.
- Crosscultural leadership development may be the most important task in missions.

This globalization of the church brings fresh challenges. Many individuals and organizations remain unaware of cultural leadership differences, often leading to confusion and bitter misunderstanding.

In spite of profound yet hidden differences, many pastors naively lead short-term teams and attempt to create crosscultural partnerships. I have noticed a growing number of voices suggesting that anyone can do crosscultural missions. Missiologists call this "the amateurization of missions," while the amateurs call it "the democratization of missions." Mission pastors rightly react against purists who would like to require that all missionaries have a doctorate in anthropology before serving in another culture. The other extreme is even more dangerous. I've heard youth pastors tell their mission team, "Just be yourself, and everyone will love you." This is a formula for crosscultural disaster. After being burned by bitter cultural misunderstandings, church leaders are recognizing the need for a deeper understanding of cultural differences in leadership.

For God's people to work together effectively, implicit assumptions about leadership need to be made explicit. They must be evaluated in light of sound social science research and biblical principles. The church in the North and South, the East and West acts out of unconscious and often confusing assumptions about leadership. We must appreciate the differences and challenge some of the misconceptions in order to work together as the worldwide body of Christ.

You don't have to travel from Australia to Afghanistan to bump into cultural leadership differences. Remarkable variations exist in the same country, even a few blocks from each other! Cultural assumptions about leadership between young business graduates and very senior executives frustrate both age groups. Those growing up in rural communities experience leadership shock when they share office space with colleagues from London, Manhattan or Lagos. Disagreements between ethnically diverse neighbors are often the result of conflicting cultural values. Several research studies indicate that women and men tend to lead with dissimilar cultural values.[1] Radical differences exist between the leadership culture of a for-profit corporation and that of a volunteer association.[2] First-generation immigrants are puzzled by the leadership expectations of second- and third-generation children. Anyone who leads or is led—in other words, everyone—is inescapably impacted by cultural assumptions about leadership.

Our global economy thrusts together people with radically divergent assumptions about leadership. Thomas Friedman writes of the fascinating manufacturing history of his Dell computer. In story after story, he describes computer components made by British-owned companies in India, China and Malaysia; by Japanese and Taiwanese and Irish-owned companies in China; by American-owned companies in Malaysia; as well as by companies in the Philippines, Costa Rica, South Korea, Thailand and Israel.[3] The globalization of business has spawned hundreds of studies investigating the effects of culture on leadership. These insightful analyses provide a rich source for forging understanding and cooperation in the global church.

Mission agencies today are increasingly and delightfully multicultural. This is a moment in history when the whole church faces an unprecedented opportunity to reach out to the whole world. I witnessed a mission team in northern India made up of Canadians, Guatemalans, Japanese, Koreans, North Americans, Ethiopians and Indians sharing the gospel with Muslims along the Ganges River. The message of the gospel takes on significant credibility when communicated by such an international team. The skeptic who says that Christianity is a Western religion must give pause when those communicating the good news come from diverse cultures. World missions must be multicultural because the gospel is for everyone and the Great Commission is for all believers. But being an effective multicultural leader is not easy, especially when false expectations and hidden assumptions exist about what it means to be a leader or follower.

Tens of millions of business people, scholars, migrants, immigrants and refugees are flooding countries that traditionally contained one or two dominant cultures. Countries such as Korea, China, Brazil, India and Nigeria are now contributing astounding numbers of missionaries worldwide.[4] This brings phenomenal opportunities for crosscultural church cooperation—along with serious challenges.

The following scenarios illustrate the interplay of leadership and culture. Some names and places have been changed, but these are actual stories from my personal experience that reflect the challenges of crosscultural leadership.

*Scenario 1: North Americans in Peru.* The short-term team from a North American church spent months preparing to partner with a church in Peru. Church leaders in Peru asked the multigenerational church team to conduct a marriage enrichment seminar. The American team recruited people who had the experience and training to teach a marriage-enrichment seminar, and they worked hard to adapt their materials to Peruvian culture. But when the Americans arrived in Peru they were told that the marriage-enrichment seminar had been cancelled. Brian was furious at the apparent dishonesty of bringing a well-trained team all the way to Peru, with all the planning, costs and time involved, just to cancel the program. But Margaret, who didn't speak a word of Spanish, decided that she would simply get to know the Peruvian family in whose home she was staying. Long into the night, she found ways to communicate, as she and her host family shared photographs and stories about their families. Margaret came back a changed person, with many new Peruvian friends. Brian came home frustrated and resentful. What was the difference? Perhaps Margaret understood that some individuals and cultures are *goal-oriented* while others are explicitly *relationship-oriented*.

*Scenario 2: Multicultural team building in Liberia.* As a silent observer, I sat in a back corner of the living room in northern Liberia and listened as missionaries discussed strategy. Tension grew as Canadians, Koreans, New Zealanders and Nigerians debated what it meant to be a team. The Nigerian missionary suggested that the team do everything together; the Korean missionary urged a daily 5 a.m. prayer meeting; and the New Zealand family suggested that a once-a-month reporting session would be enough. The Canadian was miffed at the Korean for intruding into morning family time, and the Nigerian was peeved at the New Zealander for being uncooperative. The conversation grew more strained. What was going on? Cultural values of *individualism* versus *collectivism* most often lie hidden below the surface, yet have a significant visible impact for crosscultural teams.

*Scenario 3: Long-term planning in Nigeria.* My Nigerian boss approached me with a problem. The mission had given him an ultimatum: the national church needed to produce a detailed five-year plan before the church would receive any more financial support for projects. My boss was a well-educated, bicultural person who fully understood what the mission wanted, but he wasn't convinced that a detailed five-year plan was a good idea. "We don't know what will happen to the Nigerian economy or the political situation five years from now. We don't know if there might be a 'people movement' that might call for sending Nigerian missionaries to an unexpected part of the country." He asked me to help him draw up a five-year plan that would satisfy the mission and still allow flexibility for the Nigerian church. Is such a request possible? Cultures with a *low tolerance for ambiguity* clash with those embracing a *high tolerance for ambiguity,* and this can lead to tension among leaders in planning and evaluation.

**Scenario 4: Team tensions in Uruguay.** Alejandro was a Colombian missionary happily serving in Uruguay on a church-planting team that included a South African, a Singaporean and a German. The team worked beautifully for the first year. When the church began to hold services, Alejandro was appointed to be the interim pastor until a Uruguayan could take the position. But as soon as he became the pastor, his leadership style changed and he no longer consulted with other team members or held team meetings. It seemed as if Alejandro had shifted from being an egalitarian team-player to a paternalistic leader. The high-performance multicultural team fell apart. What happened? Cultural expectations regarding perceptions of *high power distance* versus *low power distance* often lead to challenges for mission leaders in multicultural teams.

**Scenario 5: Second-generation Japanese in Chicago.** A large and growing Japanese church in Chicago called a new senior pastor from Tokyo, Japan. The church was excited to have a man who was well known as a powerful preacher and a widely respected leader. The new pastor spoke some English, but was more comfortable preaching in Japanese. Older church members had spent most of their adult years in Japan and were quite comfortable with the new pastor. But many of the middle-aged members, though born in Japan, had been in the United States for so long that their Japanese language ability was not fluent.

While they fully understood Japanese leadership values of respect and obedience, they had also become comfortable with a more egalitarian style of leadership. Their children, second-generation young people in the church, didn't speak Japanese and had profoundly absorbed the American youth culture. The senior pastor was perturbed by what he perceived as a lack of respect from the young people, while the youth seemed to be embarrassed by their "uncool" pastor who didn't know English and wanted to tell them how to run a youth group. The clash of leadership values between a *high-power-distance, collectivistic* culture and a *low-power-distance, individualistic* culture is a challenge in many immigrant churches.

## JOYS AND CHALLENGES OF MULTICULTURAL LEADERSHIP

We live in an amazing era of missions. Newly planted churches in the so-called mission-receiving countries are growing rapidly, embracing the Great Commission and sending out record numbers of their own missionaries. The slogan "from everywhere to everywhere" has become a reality where missionaries are sent from nearly every country of the world into hundreds of crosscultural settings. Following are some of the more recent developments in world missions.

*Development 1: From everywhere to everywhere.* Missionary teams venture out from many countries and cultures. While leading a vision seminar in Sudan, we met Samuel and Rebecca. Samuel, from India, is married to Rebecca, from Taiwan. Their financial support comes from churches in India, Singapore, Taiwan and Indonesia. Recently, the churches in Sudan sent out a call for a hundred teachers to come to Southern Sudan to teach the Bible and help develop church leaders who have just emerged from a decades-long civil war. SIM[5] missionaries arrived from the United Kingdom, Canada and the United States. The missionary arm of the church that relates to SIM in Nigeria dispatched twelve Nigerians, the SIM-related church in Ethiopia added eight Ethiopians, and the church in Kenya sent four Kenyans. What a joy to see missionaries from the East and West streaming forward with boldness and sacrifice to partner with missionaries in Africa to meet a desperate need for leadership development in Sudan! Such global mission teams face the challenges of different cultural assumptions about leadership. Asian leadership styles differ greatly from those in North America, and Sudanese leadership expectations differ from those of Nigeria.

*Development 2: Short-term missions.* International short-term mission teams are growing at such a rate that no one seems to be able to keep up with the numbers. Youth pastors are expected to be able to lead crosscultural mission trips if they hope to get hired or keep their jobs. Short-term missions has become a global phenomenon. Not only do several million short-term North American missionaries make yearly mission trips, but groups also go from Korea to Afghanistan, from Chile to Niger, from Guatemala to India, and so on. Again, tremendous challenges arise in the leadership functions of planning and organizing interactions between cultures. Often the short-term teams have little crosscultural experience. They are caught off guard by leadership differences in planning and implementation. At the same time, leaders receiving the short-term teams are often unprepared for clashes in cultural values. An Asian, African or Latin host might be taken back by the directness, boldness and informality of a visiting American or Australian team.

*Development 3: Church-to-church partnerships.* Church-to-church partnerships demonstrate another increasing trend. Leadership challenges emerge when churches in Taiwan, England, Colombia or the United States seek a partnership relationship with churches in cultures with radically different understandings of leadership. The very concept of "partnership" is loaded with cultural expectations that can puzzle both sides of the agreement. The idea of "equal partners" is foreign to most of the world. Partnership in much of the world assumes a junior and senior member. Usually churches from wealthy countries are expected to be the senior partner or the patron, even if they don't want to be. When a local church becomes involved in a crosscultural partnership, leaders must understand cultural differences. What are the implicit assumptions about what it means to be a leader, follower or partner?

*Development 4: Leadership development strategies.* Missiologists once defined missions solely as world evangelization, or reaching the least-reached people groups. The nurture of newly planted churches and leadership development were thought to be of secondary importance or even a distraction from "real" missions. Today, however, missiologists realize that a crucial task of world missions is the nurture and development of leaders. Whole mission agencies have sprung up with the primary objective of doing leadership training. Megachurches often conduct leadership seminars around the world. Such seminars may make the naive assumption that leadership is culture-free and that anyone from any culture can teach it. They often claim they are teaching the "biblical model" of leadership, not realizing that the way they read the Bible is already influenced by their cultural theories about leadership.

***Development 5: Working under leadership of another culture.*** In the colonial era it was assumed that the missionary would be the leader. But in today's world the expatriate missionary more often works under national church leaders, or under missionaries from countries with radically different assumptions about how to lead. For all the thirteen years my wife and I served in Nigeria with SIM, I gladly served under the leadership of Nigerian directors. But I was often caught off guard by unexpected assumptions about leadership values. I struggled to unlearn many of my hidden assumptions about leadership and to embrace new ways of leading and being led.

When I finally got my turn with my boss in his living room that evening and explained to him the urgent matter of the Bible school's imminent closing, he thought for a second and then said, "Come with me." I followed him to his office about a block away. He opened the safe and gave me a briefcase full of Nigerian currency equivalent to over 20,000 U.S. dollars. "This should be enough to keep the school open for the rest of the year," he said. I was astounded. I asked him where he got the money, and he told me that people in the United States had given it to him to build a much-needed addition to his small house, but the Bible college needed it more than his family. I asked him if he wanted a receipt, but he just waved and said, "No, I trust you." The students, teachers and board members of the Bible college were jubilant when I climbed out of the small mission airplane the following day, carrying a suitcase bulging with cash.

My gifted Nigerian supervisor taught me valuable lessons about leadership. I thought he was rude to disregard appointments; he taught me that *time* is not to be dichotomized into artificial blocks. I was embarrassed to go to his private home on official business; he taught me that location was not to be separated into official and private *space*. I assumed that money was divided into personal and business *categories;* he taught me extraordinary generosity.

### SUMMARY AND CONCLUSIONS

The glorious existence of the interconnected worldwide church compels critical reflection on leadership and culture. For the worldwide body of Christ to work in unity, we must look afresh at hidden assumptions about cultural values regarding leadership while we pursue biblical principles that affirm and challenge these values. I believe we can be both biblical and flexible in our philosophy and practice of leadership. My prayer is that leaders around the globe will humbly learn to work together as we look toward the day when people from every language, people and nation will sing hallelujahs at the wedding feast of the Lamb!

Some of my friends and mentors have agreed to contribute vignettes about what they are learning about crosscultural leadership. These reflections can be found between chapters.

In the next chapter I will discuss some of the things I am still learning about leadership. One of my friends suggested that I title the chapter "My 1001 Greatest Leadership Mistakes." I thank the Lord for those who patiently mentored me in my leadership development. Much of my philosophy of leadership has grown out of these experiences.

# REFLECTIONS ON MULTICULTURAL LEADERSHIP

Dr. Joshua Bogunjoko, Deputy International Director for SIM (Serving In Mission) with responsibility for Europe and West Africa

Crosscultural leadership has taken us beyond our own cultural pre-conception of leadership to appreciate the view of leadership from very diverse cultures. My wife, Joanna, and I are from Nigeria, and we began our missionary career as physicians in Niger. After further study in Canada, we were asked to serve in a leadership role with the international team of SIM. It has been a delight to be able to come alongside people from so many different backgrounds and cultures, working and walking together to encourage and support effective ministry.

The difficulties of working in crosscultural ministry are more or less a flip side of its delight. The different cultural understandings that bring such richness to crosscultural leadership also bring the greatest challenge. This includes balancing different ideas and ex-pectations of leadership roles among different cultural groups and even among people of similar cultural groups who do Christian leadership differently.

There is also the challenge of the language of leadership. The way people understand and interpret concepts such as servant leadership and consultative or participatory leadership all differ from culture to culture and from experience to experience. These differences are not only between people of different cultures, but also between individuals from similar cultures. Diversity of thoughts and ideas brings richness and beauty. The delight of working cross-culturally is that we get to see and know other peoples' differing ideas. Sometimes, we may actually be saying the same thing in dif-ferent ways.

Choosing to be learners is what helps us most to understand different perspectives on leadership. Crosscultural leadership is a school from which you never graduate. I don't think anyone comes to crosscultural leadership with a superior or inferior view of leadership; we just all come with different views. It is my responsibility as a leader to learn from others what their views are and why, and to help them understand where I am coming from. This can only happen by being honest about my own need to know and understand others, to be vulnerable and open, seeking to understand before trying to be understood, being an empathetic listener and showing true respect for cultural differences in leadership practices, models and styles. I need to ask clarifying questions to be sure that I am being understood, as well as to ensure that I have understood.

I have also learned that leadership in general and crosscultural leadership in particular is not about my success, but about walking with and helping others succeed, whatever their cultural peculiarities may be and whatever their callings are. It is about helping others be all that God has called them to be as much as I can help in that process. Since no condition is permanent, a follower can become a leader someday, and one needs to be prepared to accept with humility the leadership of someone who had previously worked under his or her leadership.

I have learned that there are no superior or inferior cultures or cultural approaches to leadership; there are only different approaches. No particular culture's approach is inherently bad or unbiblical, and no particular culture is completely biblical. I have learned to ask questions, to ask not only what and how, but why. The "what" helps me understand what is expected. The "how" helps me understand the culturally appropriate approach, but it is the "why" that helps me understand the culture itself. It is the "why" question that unmasks the deep cultural value behind the "what" and "how."

I confess that I owe a significant part of my growth as a Christian to opportunities to serve in leadership roles, especially crosscultural leadership. I have had opportunity to evaluate my own cultural leadership norms and my own cultural heritage. This in turn allows other cultural views to help me draw new conclusions and adopt new attitudes as I continue to learn and lead.

# MY PILGRIMAGE
# IN LEADERSHIP

*Show me a great leader, and I'll show you a hungry learner.*

Henry Blackaby

*Crosscultural leadership is a school from which you never graduate.*

Joshua Bogunjoko

When I was a young child, my strict German grandfather often reminded me, "Anything worth doing, is worth doing well." But the proverb frequently backfired. I realized that I could do few things well so I didn't even try to do them. Later in my career, my doctoral mentor, Ted Ward, modified the proverb to say, "Anything worth doing is worth doing poorly . . . the first time . . . and better the second time." He emphasized that the important lesson of that proverb is to ask, "Is it really worth doing?" And if so, "Can we learn from our mistakes?"

There is a story about a little boy from the cattle-herding Fulani people in West Africa. Like children often do on a trip, he asked his father, "How much longer until we get there?" to which his father answered, "Never. We are nomads." I used to think I would eventually master the art of multicultural leadership. Now I realize that my pilgrimage has just begun. As I look back on my life I'm amazed and embarrassed at my innocent ignorance. Yet the pilgrimage isn't over. We aren't home yet, and we must keep learning.

When we first arrived in Nigeria I was intimidated by veteran missionaries who had many years of experience. Howard Dowdell, my unofficial mentor, challenged me with the idea that "there are two kinds of missionaries—those with twenty years of experience, and those with one year of experience repeated twenty times. The difference between these two kinds of missionaries is that the first learns from experience." He helped me to see that *experience without reflection is not necessarily educational.*

While I still have much to learn about culture and leadership, I owe a debt of gratitude to those who have taught me. I'm sorry to admit that most of what I have learned about leadership and culture has come through making mistakes. I wish there were easier ways to learn, but as long as we take care to let our mistakes be instructive, we can hope to become effective crosscultural leaders.

## LEARNING TO BE A FOLLOWER

The summer after I graduated from high school, I worked at Turners Fruit Farm in Saginaw, Michigan, along with dozens of migrant workers from Mexico. At 6 a.m. every morning we became soaked in the morning dew as we picked strawberries and cucumbers and then hoed long dusty rows of sweet corn. Since I was the only one with a U.S. driver's license, I delivered the produce to grocery stores. But I quickly realized that I was not the leader. The Mexican migrant workers knew far more than I would ever learn about farming. But amazingly, they didn't criticize the "gringo kid." They graciously helped me and taught me how to work faster as I learned the trade of picking and hoeing. Each of us earned fifty cents for hoeing a quarter-mile row of sweet corn.

One hot afternoon, an elderly grandmother worked the row next to me. Since she could hoe twice as fast as I could, we would visit for a few minutes until she got so far ahead that we couldn't talk. When she got to the end of her row, she would work back on my row so we could begin the next rows together and talk some more. I was astounded. Here was an elderly Mexican migrant living below the poverty line, subsidizing a slow-working American high school kid just so we could spend a few minutes getting to know one another. These dear people taught me about a culture that valued relationships above money. I found I was quickly accepted as a friend, and I learned to be taught by people much more competent than me. My first crosscultural leadership experience taught me how to be a follower.

## WORKING FOR ETERNAL VALUES

During high school I worked at Camp Barakel in northern Michigan as an "engineer" (garbage collector and lumber jack), counselor and finally head counselor. As an engineer, I worked closely with Hiram "Hi" Johnson. Hi was an outstanding leader who had somehow learned to put up with rambunctious, immature high school boys. He demonstrated the value of hard work and the joys of finishing a task while he also taught us carpentry, roofing and bricklaying skills. But most important was his inspiration to do everything to the glory of God. He reminded us often that even the most menial work had eternal value.

One day we worked until dark trying to finish a staff house before the camp season started. My shirt was soaked with sweat, and my hands were blistered from shoveling sand around the foundation. I was beginning to feel sorry for myself when Hi Johnson strode around the corner of the building. He watched what we were doing for a while and then quietly reminded us that the staff who were moving into this house would be a big help to the camp. Then he said something I will never forget: "Your shoveling will, in the long run, be used of the Lord to bring a lot of campers to Jesus." We started shoveling with a renewed sense of purpose. Now we were not just a bunch of dirty, sweaty high school kids tired of shoveling sand. We were instruments of God Almighty to bring people to himself. What a lesson in leadership! Our view of the task shifted from shoveling sand to building the kingdom.

*all about the word you use*

## RESPECTING UNEXPECTED LEADERSHIP

After my junior year of college I spent a summer as a short-term missionary with Wycliffe Bible Translators, living among the Cashinawa Indians in the jungles of Peru. My assignment was to help clear an airstrip, and I naively assumed that I would be the leader. After only one morning swinging a machete, I learned to my chagrin that I was not the leader. In fact I was the least competent person in the village. I was just a sweaty, blistered kid standing in awe at the skills of the Cashinawa people. One day as we hiked along the jungle trails, it dawned on me that if I became separated from my new friends I could not survive more than a day. My first experience outside of the United States humbled me and taught me valuable lessons about how to follow leaders from other cultures.

## GETTING PEOPLE TO WORK TOGETHER

After graduating from Wheaton College I married my college sweetheart, Carol, and I went to work as the program director at Camp Barakel. In this role I worked closely with the director, Holman "Johnnie" Johnson, whom I had admired since I was a kid. One day I walked into his office and found him sitting behind his desk with his head in his hands. I asked, "What's the problem?" He replied, "The hardest thing about being director is working with people who don't get along with each other."

I knew Johnnie as an outstanding man of faith and vision, and it was alarming to see my leadership hero discouraged. His vision and faith seemed audacious to most people. Yet the Lord had blessed Johnnie year after year by bringing people and resources just in time for the camp to be successful. Thousands of children, youth and adults found Christ in this place, rededicated their lives to the Lord and continued to grow in their faith. The shock of seeing my hero so discouraged about the crucial leadership task of getting people to work together taught me that even the most visionary, faith-driven and successful leaders are plagued with relationship problems. I have returned to this lesson many times during my years in leadership.

## LEARNING FROM BYANG KATO

A year later, after raising support, Carol and I left Camp Barakel and traveled to Nigeria to work with what was then called the Sudan Interior Mission (SIM). I served as the director of Christian Education for the Evangelical Churches of West Africa (ECWA). Looking back I'm surprised and grateful that SIM would assign a first-term missionary with so little crosscultural experience to such a responsible leadership position. My task was to develop Christian Education curriculum for about a thousand ECWA churches. I was given a leadership title and reported directly to Dr. Byang Kato, the general director of ECWA. What an enormous privilege it was for me to travel with this godly leader and to learn fresh lessons in leadership from him. While traveling the bumpy roads of Nigeria I interviewed Byang and took copious notes about cultural practices surrounding birth, marriage, child rearing, funerals and much more. He went on to give leadership to the Association of Evangelicals of Africa, headquartered in Kenya. At the age of thirty-seven he died tragically in a drowning accident in the Indian Ocean. It was one of the saddest days for me and for all evangelicals in Africa.

## MAXIMIZING THE LEADERSHIP OF OTHERS

While Byang gave me the title of director of Christian education for ECWA, I realized that the real influencers in my learning path were my colleagues, Philip Gambo, David Buremoh and Samuila Kure. We traveled together to every church district in Nigeria, conducting five-day Sunday School conferences, eating local food and sleeping in hammocks or on church benches. I began to learn that leadership has little to do with formal titles, but with the ability to influence people. In the evening we would plan together the sessions for the next day. My Nigerian colleagues were powerful preachers, teachers and motivators. They taught me that my leadership task was to do everything I could to maximize their leadership. While I had the official leadership title, they were much more effective in ministry, and it was my job to enhance their effectiveness. After a few years, I had the delight of turning my director responsibilities over to the highly competent Samuila Kure.

## LEARNING FROM MENTORS

I am thankful for the patient way that SIM leaders Bill Crouch, Harold Fuller and Howard Dowdell mentored me. They gave me opportunities to learn and to lead beyond anything I deserved or expected. They presented me with a challenging assignment, then supported me in every way. I learned that *leadership development takes place through the challenge of problem-solving with support by mentors.*

During my first year, Howard Dowdell invited me to his office every day during the morning "tea time," a ritual left by the colonial British. He asked me questions about how I was doing and always, always what I was learning! He inquired about my goals and strategies for the development of Christian education in the churches. He never told me what to do, but his questions challenged me to rethink many of my assumptions about leadership and culture. I came away from our daily meetings with a deep sense of gratitude that a senior missionary would spend so much time with me, and also with an uneasy sense that I had a huge amount to learn. Howard taught me the value of reflective mentoring in leadership development.

## LEARNING THROUGH FORMAL EDUCATION

While serving in Nigeria, I was selected to take two courses offered by the American Management Association. The course taught that "management is the art of getting things done through other people." I studied PERT charts and planning, differences between goals and aims, and management by objectives. When I came home at night Carol would ask with a mischievous grin, "What techniques have you learned today to manipulate me into doing what you want me to do?"

I was honored to be selected for the course and studied hard. I diligently completed all the programmed instruction workbooks, participated in the case studies, and planned complicated GANT charts that included precise objectives with multiple task and timelines. But all the while something in me whispered that this teaching did not fit the Nigerian management culture and perhaps had limited application elsewhere. I had seldom seen Nigerian leaders apply the AMA management models, and sometimes this showed. From lack of planning, hospitals ran out of medicines and Bible schools opened without text-books. Yet in spite of these difficulties, the growth of the church was one of the fastest in the world. How could such outstanding church growth happen without "proper" management techniques? The AMA management course raised subtle doubts in my mind about the universal benefits of Western management models.

## PURSUING AN UNDERSTANDING OF CULTURE

While on home assignment back in the United States, I finished a master's degree at Wheaton College. Professors Lois and Mary LeBar reinforced my passion for the integration of Bible teaching and life. My understanding of culture exploded as I studied biculturalism with Marvin Mayers. He gave me a thirst to pursue an understanding of how culture impacts teaching, learning and leading.

On another home assignment I began doctoral studies at Michigan State University under the direction of Ted Ward. Ted introduced me to powerful and practical theories of culture, the dignity of persons, human development and radical views about leadership. Ted taught profoundly as a classroom teacher and also by his informal leadership example and mentoring. My studies at MSU reinforced the idea that there is nothing as practical as good theory, and nothing as impractical as practice without theory or theory without practice.

## LEADING IN CRISIS

We returned to Nigeria for what would be our final term. Our best missionary friends were Canadians Len and Luella Dyck. Len was a missionary pilot. Their children were about the same age as ours, and Len and I did all kinds of things together. We played squash, built a darkroom for photography, went camping and often flew together in small Piper airplanes. Other than my wife, Carol, Len had become the best friend I ever had.

One night as our families were eating homemade pizza together, we began to plan for a test flight the next day. The engine of the Piper had been rebuilt and needed to be tested. Because the pilot had to write data and fly at the same time, it was often best to have a second person along to record numbers. We had done many test flights together. Just as we were planning a time for the flight, a group of pastors dropped by unexpectedly for a visit. Len left and said we would work on a time for the test flight later. We never did set up a time for the flight, and Len conducted the test by himself. He never came back.

For the first two days we searched for Len's plane with over twenty small airplanes and hundreds of ground searchers. But the search was chaotic. No one knew where others had searched, we lacked topographical maps, and time was running out to rescue Len if he was injured. The top SIM leadership was out of the country, the search was in disarray, and my best friend was missing. So I took over the leadership without anyone asking me to. I called a meeting of the search pilots and those in charge of ground searches. Without official authority I began directing people to find maps, set up a sensible search plan and work together. We cancelled classes at the school for missionaries' children so that students could search large desolated areas and act as spotters in the airplanes. A week later we found the crash site and learned that Len had died instantly on impact.

I still grieve the loss of my best friend. Len's death taught me the frailty of life. I should have been on that flight with Len. The event also caused me to reflect on the change in my leadership style during those days of crisis. No longer was I a participative, people-oriented leader; I became highly directive and task-oriented. Is it possible that leadership style needs to change during a time of crisis? I began reflecting on the possibility of situational leadership.

## LEADING IN ACADEMIA

After thirteen years with SIM in Nigeria our family returned to the United States where I became a professor at Wheaton College and Graduate School. I was deeply relieved to know that the burden of leadership was no longer on my shoulders. All I had to do was teach gifted and motivated students. However, at the end of the first semester I was asked to chair the Department of Educational Ministries and, by the end of the second semester I became acting dean of Wheaton Graduate School. Once again I felt overwhelmed and incompetent for this challenge. With no experience in leading highly educated North American Ph.D.s, I needed to listen to the "natives"— the faculty and administrators. The tenured faculty reminded me that even as dean I had very little formal power. They taught me to lead by building trust and consensus. I often found myself sandwiched between highly gifted faculty (who didn't want leadership) and efficient administrators (who wanted me to bring change to the graduate school). I'm thankful for patient Wheaton colleagues who taught me about academic leadership.

## LEADING IN MISSION

After thirteen years of teaching and administration at Wheaton College, SIM (today called Serving in Mission) asked me to consider returning to the mission as the international director. This proved to be my most challenging leadership task. By this time SIM had about 1,400 missionaries from forty nationalities, working in forty-five countries. The mission had expanded into Asia and South America as well as Africa.

I distinctly remember how unready I felt to take over the top leadership of SIM. In preparation I transitioned for three months under the wise leadership of my predecessor, Ian Hay. On his last day as general director, both of us worked late into the evening. I wondered how he was feeling about leaving a distinguished career in leadership and turning it over to someone who had never held an elected position in the mission and knew so little. Just before dark Ian walked into my office. Without a word, he placed on my desk a bumper sticker that read: *The Main Thing is to keep the Main Thing the Main Thing.* He smiled and walked out. What a lesson! Ten years later, I gave the same bumper sticker to my successor, Malcolm McGregor. It seems that the "main thing" in a general mission like SIM tends to become diffuse.

A general mission does a little bit of everything and can easily lose focus. SIM flies airplanes, but it is not an aviation mission. SIM runs hospitals, but it is not a medical mission. SIM digs wells, runs agricultural projects and distributes food during times of famine, but it is not primarily a relief and development mission. SIM translates the Bible, but it is not solely a Bible translation mission. All these ministries are the primary focus of very good organizations, but they are not the core focus of a general mission like SIM. I realized that in order to "keep the main thing the main thing," we needed to refocus our mission statement. The new statement read: "SIM exists to glorify God by planting, strengthening and partnering with churches around the world." We added a list of things we do to make that vision a reality, but *the glory of God in the worldwide church* was our Main Thing. I learned that the major task of a leader is to refocus and rekindle vision.

When I took over as international director of SIM I realized that everyone who reported to me knew much more about the mission than I did. Howard Brant had deep relationships with church leaders and a passion for internationalizing missions; Eldon Howard was brilliant in understanding the complicated ins and outs of mission finances; Ron Wiebe was a wise, experienced and gracious expert on Latin America, and Gordon Stanley knew every detail of the personnel department. Looking back I'm glad it was my own healthy sense of incompetence that led me to adopt a team leadership style. I understood that I was the leader, that I had the final say in decisions, but I also realized that my primary task was to do everything possible to facilitate the leadership of the deputy directors. I sensed that my job was to *harmonize, enhance and focus the leadership gifts of others in working toward a common vision for SIM.* Those who reported to me taught me that "in the multitude of counselors there is safety" (Prov 11:14 KJV).

## LEARNING FROM CRITICISM

One day a good friend walked into my SIM office and began a tirade of criticism. As he went on and on for almost an hour, I became more and more irritated and annoyed. Finally I asked him, "Why are you doing this?" He answered, "The Lord has given me the gift of criticism." Never before had I been in a job where I had been lambasted like this. I was seldom criticized as a missionary in Nigeria or as a professor at Wheaton. Possibly Nigerians were too polite to be so overtly judgmental of the missionary. As a professor, some students complained that my assignments were too long, but I jokingly reminded them that with tuition going up every year, they were still reading the same number of pages per dollar. Now I found that the international director was open for criticism from around the world.

While critics can cause much harm, they can also be good teachers. There is usually at least a kernel of truth (and sometimes a bushel full!) in each criticism. Critics reminded me about my frailty and were used of the Lord to humble me whenever I thought I might be a great leader. I was criticized less than I deserved. Critics also taught me to trust the Lord in the discouragements of leadership. Before he finished his tenure as general director, Ian Hay gave his leadership team a bronze plaque that read, *"I steadfastly refuse to gratify the Devil by becoming discouraged."* I kept this plaque on the keyboard of my computer during my ten years as international director.

### TRUSTING ONSITE LEADERSHIP

On my first day in office I received a telephone call from northern Kenya telling me of a gun battle where a UN worker was killed. The missionaries were asking what to do. A couple of years later I received a 2 a.m. phone call from Liberia reporting that the two remaining missionaries at the ELWA radio station had endured wave after wave of looting throughout the night, and they were walking barefoot, trying to get to the U.S. embassy. What did I recommend? I realized that in times of crisis we needed to trust the Lord and we also needed emergency plans. But I also learned that it is difficult to make decisions for Africa while sitting in an air-conditioned office seven thousand miles away. I needed to trust the Lord, and I also needed to trust the leadership close to the situation.

It seems that the temptation is for field leaders to delegate decisions upward and for international leaders to micromanage the fields. For example, I received a phone call from a director in East Africa asking me if he could buy four new tires for his Land Rover. I was tempted to ask him some pseudo-wise questions about his budget and then pontificate a decision. Email makes it all the more easy to manage from the top. Crisis situations and a God-given clarity about my inadequacies taught me that decisions need to be made close to where they will be carried out.

## LEADING WITH VISION

I learned that change can't be forced in an organization made up of hundreds of volunteers from forty countries. Top-down change doesn't work with independent missionaries who are technically self-employed. But we worked to create an atmosphere of change centered around a compelling vision. I also learned to appreciate leaders at every level of the organization who were possibility thinkers. The biggest difference between a stagnant field and a dynamic one seemed to be the vision of the leader and the ability of that leader to build a team of people who could also catch the vision. My experience as international director taught me about the strategic difference between effective and ineffective leaders and that the right directors can make a significant difference for the whole country.

While I served as international director, SIM merged with Africa Evangelical Fellowship, which had ministries in fourteen countries. China, Ecuador, Chile, Paraguay and Uruguay were also added as new ministry areas. Korea and South Africa joined SIM as sending countries and joint owners of the mission. We realized that if we were to be truly international we would need to make it possible for missionaries from the less wealthy countries to join as full members, and we would need to create partnerships with dozens of organizations. We would need to blur the distinction between a sending country and a field country. For example, SIM had an effective field ministry in Ecuador, but now a Sending Council was also needed to facilitate mobilization of Ecuadorian missionaries. To do this we would need to radically change our "sacred cow"—the financial support system. We would also need to change many of the rules of the mission that reflected the values of Western sending countries.

My years as international director also drove home to me again the remarkable capacity of women in leadership. The mission did not have a precedent of women at its top leadership levels, but when positions became open, I tried to choose the best person for the job, regardless of gender. Our work in Sudan and India had stagnated with discouraged missionaries overwhelmed by political pressure and religious tensions until the appointment of women directors in both countries brought renewed vision and vitality. Many other gifted women served in various leadership capacities at every level. I knew we needed the gifts of all our members, and that women make some of the best leaders. The opportunity to choose the best person for the role, whether male or female, greatly enhanced the effectiveness of our ministries.

## LEADING THROUGH TEACHING

After two five-year terms as international director of SIM, I am now teaching again, this time at Trinity Evangelical Divinity School. Gifted students from around the world are teaching me about leadership as I have the opportunity to interact with them and challenge them about missions, education and leadership. I am again convinced that the interaction between scholarship and experience is essential in leadership.

I have served on several boards of educational institutions. I learned a great deal during my time as a board member at the Campus Crusade International School of Theology, working with visionaries such as Bill Bright and Steve Douglas as well as experienced leaders like Ted Engstrom. They taught me how a board can be both visionary and responsible without taking the leadership function away from academic leaders. I served for three years on the board of another school in the southern part of the United States. The board asked me not to serve for a second term, and I painfully learned that there was much about southern culture and leadership that I didn't understand. I am still reflecting on my leadership style on that board and also about the cultural leadership ethos of that school. I learned that some of the trickiest crosscultural challenges can occur within what we think is our own culture, but in reality is a unique subculture. Currently I am a trustee at Wheaton College, where I am learning from women and men who are gifted businesspeople, pastors, lawyers, writers and teachers. I stand in awe of the wisdom of this board and trust I will continue to learn about kingdom leadership from these colleagues.

## CONCLUSIONS

I'm glad I didn't write this book forty years ago, and I'm not sure that I'm ready yet. I suspect that the Lord still has much to teach me about leadership and culture. I hope I have forty years of experience, rather than one year of experience repeated forty times. As I look back on my life, I wish I had learned lessons more quickly without making so many mistakes. If leadership is worth doing, it is worth doing poorly . . . the first time, while learning along the way. I am grateful to all those who have been patient with me and who have taught me about leadership. In brief, these are some of the main leadership lessons the Lord has taught me through his people and through experience:

- Mexican migrant workers taught me that leadership is not about position but about relationships.

- Hiram Johnson at Camp Barakel taught me the dignity of hard work that is vision-driven and done for the Lord.

- Johnnie Johnson showed me the importance of being a visionary possibility-thinker in the midst of personnel problems.

- Byang Kato and my ECWA Nigerian colleagues taught me that the task of leadership involves maximizing the gifts of others.

- Howard Dowdell and other SIM leaders taught me how to learn from reflecting carefully on experience.

- The American Management Association course taught me both the value and the limited global applicability of North American management techniques.

- Ted Ward and other academic mentors challenged me to embrace critical reflection and taught me the practical value of good theory.

- Len Dyck's death brought home to me the fragility of life and the need for flexible leadership styles.

- My experience as academic dean of Wheaton Graduate School taught me the value of building trust and consensus among peers.

- My tenure as international director of SIM taught me the value of keeping the main thing the main thing, of focusing a team, of women in leadership, of the need for crosscultural flexibility in leadership styles and the realization that criticism is to be expected in leadership.

- All of my experiences taught me that there are many forms of leadership, and that God can give us grace to function and grow under each.

I thank the Lord for gracious leadership mentors, and pray I will continue to learn from fellow pilgrims on the path of life. I encourage each of you who are reading this book to seek out leadership mentors and intentionally reflect on your experience to learn from them.

# WHY CROSSCULTURAL LEADERSHIP?

*The servant-leader is servant first.*

ROBERT K. GREENLEAF

ELIZABETH INVESTED HER GIFTS and energies in developing leaders for camping ministries in Latin America. Then she took a study leave. Her studies in graduate school revolutionized her thinking about leadership development and she couldn't wait to get back. But one day she came to my office in tears. Her only supporting church had just dropped her funding, jeopardizing her career as a missionary. When I asked why, she told me that the missions committee of the church attended a seminar where they learned that their church needed to

1. support missionaries who had precise, measurable goals for their ministry;

2. designate all church funding to missionaries working in North Africa, the Middle East and Asia (i.e., the 10/40 Window);

3. make sure their missionaries were assigned to pioneer evangelism among least-reached people groups.

Elizabeth didn't fit any of the criteria. Fortunately, friends in the church convinced the missions committee that her ministry was strategic and that the ideas they had learned in the seminar were short-sighted. The church recommitted to her support, and Elizabeth went back to a powerful ministry of leadership development. She has produced camping curriculum and leadership training materials that have had wide impact across Latin America.

In this chapter we will reflect on the importance of crosscultural leadership development in the worldwide church. Some missiologists and mission executives either overlook or downplay the significance of developing leaders as a missionary task. I will make the case that leadership development is at the heart of world missions. We will look at the big picture of the missionary enterprise.

Missions is the crosscultural task of making disciples of Jesus. Some pastors and missionaries define missions solely as world evangelization. Yes, giving everyone an opportunity to clearly hear the good news of Jesus is of utmost importance. Evangelism is a critical component of making disciples. Charlie Davis, the international director of TEAM, makes the radical statement that "making disciples begins long before a person becomes a believer."[1] I'm convinced that missions begins with evangelism and must move to church planting, discipleship, theological education, leadership development and partnership in world missions. Fostering the development of leaders is a critical aspect of world missions. The apostle Paul spent the majority of his missionary career developing leaders in newly planted churches.

Figure 3.1 illustrates the healthy cycle of world missions. The ultimate vision is God's glory in the worldwide church, now and throughout eternity. The path illustrates a lifelong faith journey made up of thousands of small steps, divided into five stages: pre-evangelism, evangelism, church planting, leadership development and partnering in world missions.

This is a supernatural process from start to finish. Human beings do not convert people, plant churches or make leaders. All of this is the work of God's Spirit. We work *with* the Holy Spirit to introduce people to Jesus so they may grow and bring glory to the Father. The church is

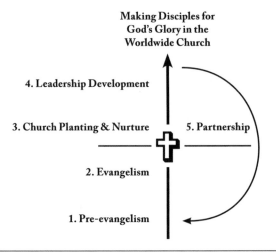

Figure 3.1. The cycle of world missions

the body of Christ established and led by him. The realization that God is in control of the spiritual development of his people is both humbling and encouraging: humbling because we are not as influential as we might think, and encouraging because the Lord of the universe is personally involved in each stage of the journey toward Christlikeness. We can't boast, but neither can we fail.

## THE ULTIMATE VISION OF MISSIONS
## THE ENDPOINT OF THE ARROW

The ultimate vision of world missions is the glory of God in the worldwide church—in this present world and in the world to come. Each stage on the arrow is a necessary and vital facet of missions, contributing toward the ultimate end. This magnificent vision is not controlled by people; it is neither predictable nor quantifiable. It will not be completed by the year 2020 or 2050 or any target date. The task of world missions will not be finished until the return of Christ.

All of Scripture points to the glorious endpoint of Christlike people from every nation singing a new song of praise to God. From Genesis to Revelation, from creation to the new creation, the primary theme of Scripture is the story of God's passion for the whole world. God created human beings to love him, rejoice in him and bring him glory. But the human race rebelled against its creator. The biblical narrative from Genesis to Revelation sings out the good news of redemption for all nations.

Let's recap some key passages:

- God chose Abram and blessed him so that he would be *a blessing to all peoples of the earth* (Gen 12:3).

- God brought the people of Israel out of Egypt and carried them on eagle wings as his treasured possession so that they might be *a kingdom of priests to the nations* (Ex 19:4-6).

- God called Isaiah to be a light to the Gentiles so that his salvation might reach the *ends of the earth* (Is 49:6).

- God's passion for his glory among the nations rings clearly through the Psalms, "May the peoples praise you, God; *may all the peoples praise you*" (Ps 67:3, italics added).

- As Jesus ascended into heaven, he commissioned his disciples to make disciples *in all the world* by going, baptizing and teaching them to obey everything Jesus commanded (Mt 28:18-20).

- The apostle Paul made many missionary journeys proclaiming the gospel and establishing churches, but he spent most of his missionary career encouraging churches to grow in grace and stay true to the teachings of Jesus.

- "Christ loved the church and gave himself up for her to make her holy, cleansing her by the washing with water through the word, and to present her to himself as *a radiant church*, without stain or wrinkle or any other blemish, but holy and blameless" (Eph 5:25-27, italics added).

- Paul was also intentional about developing leaders God had already gifted: Christ himself "gave the apostles, the prophets, the evangelists, the pastors and teachers, to *equip his people for works of service*, so that the body of Christ may be built up until we all reach unity in the faith and in the knowledge of the Son of God and *become mature, attaining to the whole measure of the fullness of Christ*" (Eph 4:11-13, italics added).

The scope of missions requires evangelism and church planting, but it doesn't stop there. Discipleship toward maturity and Christlikeness is an ongoing, lifelong process. The climax of the biblical saga is holy people of God from every nation and language standing before the throne, singing "praise and glory and wisdom and thanks and honor and power and strength be to our God for ever and ever. Amen!" (Rev 7:12). The ultimate purpose of world missions will finally be fulfilled when the great multitude from every nation, tribe, people and language join in the Hallelujah Chorus at the wedding feast of the Lamb (Rev 19:6-7). We see this vision unfolding in beautiful ways today around the world.

Figure 3.2 illustrates how the whole scope of missions fits together:

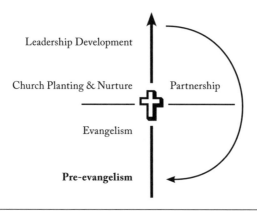

**Figure 3.2**

## PRE-EVANGELISM

In Sierra Leone, seven-year-old Hawa developed a disfiguring facial tumor. Her father, Hassan, struggled to make a living by digging for small diamonds to sell. As he tried to protect his sick child from those who taunted her, life became increasingly difficult for this Muslim family. Hassan took his daughter to a hospital, where doctors gave him little hope. She needed a surgeon. When Hassan heard of the Mercy

Ship in neighboring Liberia, he decided to make the difficult two-day trip to Monrovia. It was his daughter's only hope. After three hours of surgery, followed by time on the ward, Hawa and Hassan returned to Sierra Leone. Hassan is now thinking deeply about the person called Jesus whom he heard about on board a big ship.[2]

Kindness in the name of Christ can nudge people like Hassan from antagonism to curiosity along the spiritual path. This is pre-evangelism.

Missionaries sometimes become discouraged after giving many years of loving, quiet witness without seeing anyone make a decision to follow Christ. But even small steps are significant. In countries where an overt gospel witness is difficult, people see God's love through medical work, humanitarian relief, schools and development programs.

The purpose of meeting human need is twofold: to express genuine love for people and to care about their eternal souls. Ministering to peoples' need is both an end and a means. Holistic ministry must include care for the soul as well as care for physical needs; if not, it isn't truly holistic.

While pre-evangelism is necessary, it must lead to the next step of inviting people to come to Jesus. Both "presence evangelism" and "proclamation evangelism" are needed in drawing people to Jesus.

### EVANGELISM

Every human being needs the opportunity to hear and understand the wonderful good news of Jesus. The *evangel* is the good news that "God so loved the world that he gave his one and only Son, that whoever

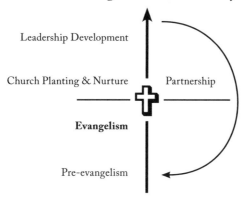

Figure 3.3

believes in him shall not perish but have eternal life" (Jn 3:16).

> Simon Chavez grew up in a Quechua family with eight children. His parents worked hard in farming, but were very poor. Simon had to leave school after fifth grade to work with his brothers in cotton farming. At age 20 he began working on the farm of a pastor, who was different from any other boss he had known. He paid him fairly and didn't cheat anyone. Simon started going to worship meetings in the pastor's home. He paid attention to the Bible teaching because he respected the pastor. In time he realized he was a sinner and asked Christ to save him from his sins. Returning to his own village, he walked four hours to church every Sunday and eventually went to a Bible Institute in the city of Sucre. Now he is presenting Quechua radio programs to help others come to Jesus.[3]

Evangelism is inviting people to come to Jesus, sharing the good news "that Christ died for our sins according to the Scriptures, that he was buried, that he was raised on the third day according to the Scriptures" (1 Cor 15:3-4). The good news is more wonderful than anyone can imagine. The God of all creation, the God who made every cell in every human being, loves us so much that he died to take away the sin that poisons us and separates us from our loving heavenly Father. The clear proclamation of the gospel is at the very heart of missions.

The apostle Paul explained God's call for him to evangelize like this:

> I will rescue you from your own people and from the Gentiles. I am sending you to them to open their eyes and turn them from darkness to light, and from the power of Satan to God, so that they may receive forgiveness of sins and a place among those who are sanctified by faith in me. (Acts 26:17-18)

Missionary experts debate the meaning of the term *evangelized*. When are people evangelized? Which people groups are evangelized and which are not evangelized? Some say that people are evangelized when they hear the gospel clearly and have an opportunity to respond. But from the journey perspective, people are not evangelized until they cross the line from death to life, from darkness to light, from the power of Satan to the power of God. What a joyful transformation!

## CHURCH PLANTING AND NURTURE

When people cross the line between darkness and light through belief in Christ, they are born again. The whole family of God rejoices at the birth of a baby, and the angels of heaven join the party. The birthing process may take a long time, accompanied by birth pains. This birth is the beginning of a brand new life. The baby Christian has now joined

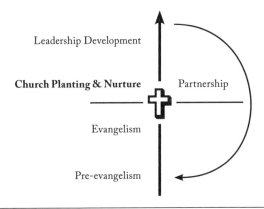

**Figure 3.4**

a new family made up of followers of Jesus from around the word, including all those who are now with Christ in heaven.

Newborns can't live for more than a few hours without the help of the family. In the same way, new believers depend on the family of God to survive. The planting, nurture and development of the people of God—his church—is essential.

Just as it is grossly irresponsible for a mother to abandon a newborn, it is indefensible for missionaries or pastors to bring people to Jesus without connecting them to the family of God. Evangelism without discipleship is like giving birth and then leaving the baby in a dumpster. Missionaries doing evangelism and those nurturing new believers are of equal importance.

Dietrich Bonhoeffer warned about the peril of ignoring radical obedience to the Lord. He wrote, "Costly grace [is] turned into cheap grace without discipleship."[4] I wonder if a myopic missionary model has contributed to cheap grace in a worldwide church that has sometimes been evangelized without discipleship.

The history of the Tamajaq people in West Africa is a sobering reminder of the crucial need for discipleship. Renowned as "warriors of the desert," the Tamajaq follow Islam. But it was not always so. The cross appears in all their arts and crafts, a subtle reminder of their Christian past in North Africa centuries ago. Now they are again learning about Christ's love for them, and some are responding. The Tamajaq, and hundreds of other groups like them, scream out the need to disciple new believers faithfully so that never again will the whole group need to be re-evangelized.

How can new believers be discipled effectively? Sue Eckert and her husband, Tim, work among the Wodaabe people in Niger, West Africa. As Sue was home schooling her own children, she included the Nicene Creed in the curriculum. "Wouldn't it be great," mused Sue "if all Wodaabe believers could declare their faith so concisely and confidently?" A local church leader translated the creed into Fulfulde, the language of the Wodaabe people, and Sue printed it on cloth banners. Then she started a Bible club for the children of the community. The children received notebooks and wrote, "I believe in God, the Father Almighty, Maker of heaven and earth." Sue and her Nigerian colleague taught from Genesis 1 and led the children in songs, prayer, and Bible memory about the Creator God. Then the following week they moved to the next lesson: "and in His Son, Jesus Christ." Step-by-step discipleship that teaches "everything Jesus commanded" is essential in the scope of missions.[5]

The apostle Paul worked hard nurturing the churches he helped to plant. It seems that the natural tendency for newly planted churches is to regress. The churches in Galatia quickly fell into legalism, and in Corinth they began to bicker over leadership. False teachers threatened the churches. Paul visited the churches again and again, challenging them to defend the truth of Christ's gospel. He wrote letters to the churches and sent other leaders to encourage the new churches. Just as Paul spent most of his ministry nurturing churches, church development should be high on the agenda of modern missionaries.

## LEADERSHIP DEVELOPMENT

The Holy Spirit gives all the gifts necessary to provide leadership for his people. In an important sense, *God is the only leader.* We are his disciples, his followers, his servants.

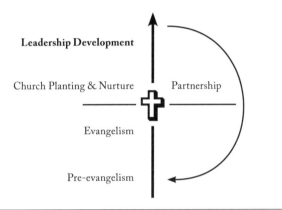

**Figure 3.5**

Newly planted churches are filled with spiritually gifted people who are commanded to use their gifts for the building up of the body of Christ. Missionaries are called to help "fan into flame" the gifts God has given his church. Leaders are needed to teach and nurture the church.

Leadership development has always been at the heart of God's redemption plan. Jesus taught and healed the sick, but his lasting ministry came from the training of the twelve disciples. Jesus was intentional about developing disciples by prayerfully selecting them, spending extra teaching time alone with them, giving them special explanations about his teaching, taking them on field trips and sending them out two-by-two in ministry. Just before the Lord ascended into heaven he commissioned his disciples to take his teaching to the ends of the earth. Leadership development for world missions was a high priority for Jesus.

Leadership development of men and women was also a cornerstone of the apostle Paul's ministry. Since we know of no occasion when Paul traveled by himself, it seems that he continually had a double objective:

planting churches and developing missionary leaders. Eckhard Schnabel, professor of New Testament at Trinity Evangelical Divinity School, writes, "Of the approximately one hundred names that are connected with Paul in the book of Acts and in the Pauline letters, thirty-eight people are coworkers of the apostle."[6] He estimates that 18 percent of Paul's coworkers were women.[7]

Contextualized theology is impossible without the development of leaders. Over a hundred and fifty years ago Rufus Anderson and Henry Venn proposed that mature churches are characterized as self-propagating, self-supporting and self-governing. The late professor of missiology at Trinity Evangelical Divinity School, Paul Hiebert, added another characteristic: that they be *self-theologizing*.[8] A healthy church must have leaders with a deep understanding of Scripture and how it should be applied to the cultural situation.

The development of *The Africa Bible Commentary*[9] is an outstanding example of "self-theologizing" in the African church. This one-volume commentary was written by seventy African scholars. The table of contents lists topics such as ancestor worship, HIV-AIDS, initiation rites and polygamy. This rich resource is important for the worldwide church, not just for Africa. As we see gifted theologians applying the Bible to African cultural issues, we are challenged to look more closely at our own. For instance, the blending of Christian doctrine with animist religion in Africa is called syncretism.[10] But what about the syncretism in our own culture? We don't see the ways we blend Christian doctrine with materialism, consumerism and individualism. African theologians can help us to see Scripture more clearly in our cultural context.[11]

So the development of leaders must be of highest priority in the scope of world missions. When people come to Christ, are nurtured in the church and develop as leaders, the glory of God is reflected through the worldwide church.

## PARTNERSHIP IN WORLD MISSIONS

The worldwide church is large and growing, and newly planted churches are catching the vision for global missions. We celebrate the joy of nations from all over the world rising up to take their mission responsibility seriously.

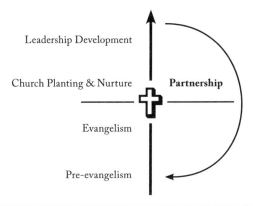

**Figure 3.6**

Missionaries by the thousands are now sent "from everywhere to everywhere." In today's world, every nation is both a mission field and a sending country. This movement—like the birth of modern missions two centuries ago—is characterized by vision, faith and sacrifice.

- In Guatemala City I listened to the heart-cry of a couple dozen young people telling of their hopes and dreams of being missionaries to the Muslim world. When it came my turn to speak I was too choked with emotion to talk.

- In Jos, Nigeria, Panya Baba challenged believers with their obligation to take the gospel around the world. After the sermon, scores of Nigerians flocked to the podium indicating their desire to serve crossculturally.

- In Jakarta, Indonesia, Chinese pastors displaced from their own country discussed their missionary vision for Muslims in their community and around the world. They are using their resources to support ministries in Sudan and northern India.

- At a missions consultation in England, a Sudanese pastor described the bulldozing of their churches in Khartoum, and then went on to list all the unreached people groups they were hoping to reach with the gospel. I was astonished and humbled that churches on the verge of extinction could have such a vision for world missions.

While these brothers and sisters possess the tenacity to serve, they are often hindered by inadequate infrastructures. They sometimes lack crosscultural training, member care and support from their home church. Many lament the marginalization that threatens to limit mission candidates sent from less affluent countries. In response to these challenges, Tabitha Plueddemann writes: "Yet, paradoxically, a perch on the periphery can be rich in opportunities. Ministry from the fringe, where few resources and no precedent exists, means that visionaries are both freed and forced to innovate. Having no script to follow, new strategies emerge from the fires of sacrifice and rivers of prayer."[12]

Both established and emerging missions can encourage each other. Partnership in world missions brings the church full circle. Partnership demonstrates what happens in the healthy scope of global missions where leadership training is a priority. This partnership then becomes the most effective way of evangelizing the unreached! Leadership training leads to partnership in mission. It doesn't compete with evangelism, but makes it even more effective.

As each generation grows and develops, they contribute new ways to shape how evangelism, discipleship, church planting and leadership development are done. Thus as global partnership and leadership are developed, the overall church learns better ways to do mission at every step of the process.

It is quite possible that the apostle Paul would not meet the qualifications of many missions committees today. He was motivated by the vision he received on the road to Damascus, but he never formulated precise measurable objectives. He devoted his energy to evangelism, but he spent the vast majority of his time planting and strengthening churches while he developed leaders and partnered with these leaders in more church planting.

Remember the opening story of Elizabeth who trains leaders for camping ministries in Latin America? The best strategy for church mission committees who care about the unreached may be to send missionaries like Elizabeth to do leadership development! God is mobilizing his church in Latin America to reach the Muslim world and other unreached groups throughout the world.

## SUMMARY

Leadership development and the making of disciples is at the heart of the missionary enterprise. If the mission enterprise neglects the development of leaders, the newly planted church will be hampered in continuing the discipleship cycle of pre-evangelism, evangelism, church planting, theological education and missions.

# REFLECTIONS ON
# MULTICULTURAL LEADERSHIP

Tim Fellows, Ethiopia

As long as I live, I will never forget the sacrificial commitment of my Ethiopian brothers to growing as leaders.

Four years ago I started a two-year leadership training program for rural church leaders. Those who attended were elders, pastors and evangelists. All were farmers with education ranging from fourth grade to tenth grade. With farming and family obligations, they did not have much of a chance to go away to Bible school.

Our program included TEE (Theological Education by Extension) courses covering Old Testament, New Testament and Bible Doctrine. We also had a seminar together every three months. The church leaders were responsible for covering the cost of transport to the seminar as well as food costs. They slept on the floor of the church—so no charge for that. I assisted by supplying the TEE books.

Amazingly, some of these leaders walked up to twelve hours to reach the seminar site!

Not long after we began the course, the local government initiated a new law demanding that each farmer be on his farm working from Monday to Friday. Inspectors were hired to enforce the law. If a farmer was absent from his farm, he was fined 15 Ethiopian burr (equivalent to almost $2.00—or two days' wage) for each day he was missing.

Since the seminars were held from Friday to Sunday, it usually meant the church leaders would miss two days, Thursday and Friday. The new rule created a lot of concern. "Could the seminars be held only on Saturday and Sunday?" We talked about the difficulty of getting adequate training in just one-and-a-half days.

After much discussion, one of the church leaders got up and said, "All of my life I have wanted a chance to study God's Word. This is the chance, and it might never come again. I don't care how much they fine me. . . . I will come." The others quickly agreed that training was such a high value to them that they would rather be fined than miss an opportunity to learn. So the training program continued—and God worked so that not one of the farmers was ever fined for being absent from his fields to attend a seminar!

# PART II

# LEADERSHIP AND CULTURE

PART TWO INVESTIGATES SOME OF THE current research describing the impact of culture on leadership values. Researchers in the business world have spent lifetimes and astounding amounts of money to discover differences in cultural values. It makes good sense for leaders in the global church to pay attention to these studies to learn how God might have designed cultural differences in believers from every nation, tribe, people and language.

# LEADERSHIP, CULTURAL VALUES
# AND THE BIBLE

*God's grace is present in all people and cultures.*
*As we submit ourselves to learning from other cultures, we catch glimpses*
*of God's grace that would be unavailable in our own culture.*

DUANE ELMER, *CROSS-CULTURAL CONFLICT*

HANS IS A SWISS MISSIONARY SERVING IN TOGO. He works with Pastor Luka planning an AIDS ministry in the capital city of Lomé. Tensions appear right from the start. Hans has designed a twelve-month flow chart with a timeline for equipment, funding and personnel. Pastor Luka wants the center to open next month. He assumes that everything will fall into place without needing to plan every detail. Pastor Luka wants to appoint a cousin to be the director—a man with a charismatic personality who is deeply respected by the community. Hans insists they appoint a director with medical and administrative experience. Pastor Luka assumes that the director will need a new car so that the AIDS center will gain the respect of the community, while Hans strongly objects to such extravagant spending. The points of conflict go on and on. What's more, both Hans and Pastor Luka are quick to cite Bible verses for their positions.

What is happening here? Hans thinks that Pastor Luka doesn't know how to plan ahead, that he's not interested in competent administration and that he spends money irresponsibly. Pastor Luka thinks that Hans doesn't trust the Lord in his planning. He doesn't understand why Hans wants to put a cold, impersonal administrator in charge of the project or why he doesn't want the center to have the respect of the community.

The illustration would become even more complicated if this team in Togo were composed of missionaries from Switzerland, Ghana, the United States, France, Ethiopia and Australia—a likely scenario in today's globalized world. Culturally diverse leadership expectations are a challenging reality in current mission teams. An understanding of cultural values and biblical leadership principles may not guarantee harmonious relationships, but it is a healthy first step.

These guidelines can help resolve leadership tensions in multicultural teams:

1. *Uncover your own unconscious cultural values.* Since we seldom reflect on our underlying values, we assume everyone thinks like we do. And we imagine that anyone who reasons differently is incompetent, rude or not raised "properly." As a new missionary, I was sitting at a meal with a group of Nigerian pastors, and realized that they didn't take off their hats. In my mind, I could hear my mother's chiding, "No eating with your hat on!" I foolishly assumed that all good mothers insist that children take off their hats during meals and found myself thinking my pastor friends were impolite. I soon learned otherwise. (And today we live in a new era of rules about hats at the table in my own culture.)

2. *Discover the cultural values of others.* Realize that others also hold values they naively assume to be universal. Most likely people are not trying to be rude when they do things differently from you. I sheepishly laughed inside as it struck me that Nigerian mothers might have taught different table manners to their children, and my pastor friends might think *me* impolite for eating with my hat off!

3. *Look for biblical principles of leadership in all of Scripture.* It's easy to find verses to prove any style of leadership. We are all attracted unknow-

ingly to parts of Scripture that are most in line with our subconscious cultural values. We don't consciously try to proof-text Bible verses, but often we do. For instance, many Bible teachers use Nehemiah as an ideal model of leadership. Someone looking for biblical proof for extreme authoritarian leadership could quote Nehemiah when he said, "I rebuked them and called curses down on them. I beat some of them and pulled out their hair" (Neh 13:25). On the other hand, a person with egalitarian leadership values might quote the apostle Paul, "I will boast all the more gladly about my weaknesses. . . . I delight in weaknesses, in insults, in hardships, in persecutions, in difficulties. For when I am weak, then I am strong" (2 Cor 12:9-10). Both authoritarian and egalitarian cultures can find biblical evidence for their opposing leadership values.

Biblical principles of leadership need to come from the whole of Scripture. Leaders in multicultural situations have the opportunity to explore Scripture from the perspective of the other culture. As we study the whole of Scripture we will find examples of leadership values that support differing views. We then seek a synthesis of *principles* rather than a proof-text of examples. Implicit biblical principles are embedded behind explicit Bible stories. One universal biblical principle is that leaders should love and care for those whom they lead. Jesus commanded us to love our neighbors as ourselves.

## THE PARADOX OF BIBLE AND CULTURE

Crosscultural leaders face a theological paradox. God is at work in every culture, but Satan is too. So examples of both good and bad leadership are found in every culture.

The image of God can be found in every culture, but the effects of our depravity are also evident. Leadership styles in every culture have the potential of reflecting good or evil in the heart of the leader. Leaders in every culture tend toward the sin of pride. Because of our fallen nature, "Power tends to corrupt, and absolute power corrupts absolutely."[1] This is true in all cultures. Competing principles of love and selfishness are at work in human hearts and are evidenced in varied leadership styles. A paternalistic leader might be selfless and loving, while an egalitarian leader might be manipulative and self-seeking.

Since we live in a fallen world, we must view with suspicion our own assumptions about leadership. Neither should we romanticize leadership styles in other cultures. I have heard missionaries declare that individualism is evil and collectivism is biblical. But the opposite is equally defensible—that collectivism leads to tribal conflict and stifles the development of individuals. In reality, good and bad motivations operate in both individualistic and collectivistic cultures.

The theological paradox reminds us that neither ethnocentrism nor cultural relativism is an adequate answer. Ethnocentrism assumes that one's own culture is the best and that other cultures are inferior. Cultural relativism presupposes that every culture is inherently noble. Both ethnocentrism and relativism overlook sinfulness rampant in every culture. Both are dismally inadequate.

To begin to resolve dilemmas of multicultural leadership we need to dig below the surface of visible external culture to investigate these questions:

- What are my underlying cultural assumptions about leadership?
- What are the underlying assumptions of those from different cultures?
- Which biblical principles of leadership must be followed in every culture?
- When does leadership need to change in order to reflect biblical principles?
- When does the Bible allow for flexibility in leadership style?

The relationship between these questions can be seen in the following diagram. The diagram illustrates that

1. No culture can boast of leadership values that are completely biblical.

2. All cultures are blessed with some biblical leadership values.

3. Cultures exhibit many differences in leadership values.

4. Cultures have some leadership values in common with other cultures.

5. Most cultures contain leadership values that intersect with those of other cultures and also follow biblical principles.

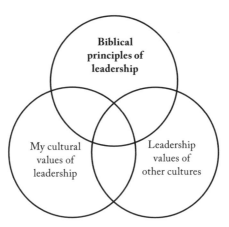

**Figure 4.1**

## BIBLICAL PRINCIPLES OF LEADERSHIP

It's not as easy as it might seem to derive biblical principles of leadership from biblical examples. The Bible is filled with hundreds of examples of leadership, and most of them are bad. Are biblical descriptions of leadership prescriptions for leaders today?[2] No. Anyone can prove any view of leadership with this method. It would be easy for Attila the Hun, Adolf Hitler, Idi Amin and Chairman Mao to find biblical examples to support their leadership styles. Jesus demonstrated a dictatorial leadership style when he overturned the tables of money changers as he drove them out of the temple with a whip (Jn 2:15). Too many Christian books on leadership are written from a monocultural perspective interspersed with Bible verses and marketed as universal biblical principles of leadership.

We all need a deep sense of humility when it comes to propounding biblical principles of leadership for other cultures. The biblical text is inspired by God and is without error, but my interpretation is not. Biblical principles of leadership are always hypotheses rather than inerrant truth. We will always see biblical principles of Scripture through the eyeglasses of our culture. Yet all human beings are created in the image of God, and the Bible is God-breathed and intended for all nations. The Spirit of God is at work in believers in every culture. So while

seeking to avoid cultural arrogance, we are grateful to God for his revealed Word to all people of all cultures. Crosscultural principles of
leadership, while tentative, are possible. Without the Bible—God's
revelation to all people—and the Holy Spirit, given to all believers, no
hope exists for the worldwide body of Christ to work together through
common principles of leadership.

As we study the biblical narrative and theology, we discover principles of leadership that are applicable across cultures. To illustrate, let's
look at an Old Testament story in Exodus 32. We read that God is
about to destroy Israel for making the golden calf and Moses is pleading with God to forgive his peoples' sin. He even tells God to blot his
own name out of the book if he will only forgive his chosen people.
Later God promises Moses, "My Presence will go with you, and I will
give you rest" (Ex 33:14).

At least three levels emerge in this story. At the *external level* we see
a discouraged Moses pleading and weeping for sinful Israel. At the
deepest *core of theology* we learn about the nature of God—a holy God
who punishes sin, but is also loving and merciful. We also learn about
the nature of human beings—created in the image of God, loved by
God, forgiven by God, and yet with a natural inclination toward evil

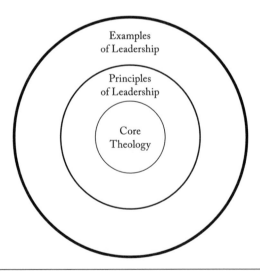

Figure 4.2

and rebellion. (We will look more deeply at the theology of leadership in chapter eleven.) In the middle are *principles of leadership.* We can safely hypothesize that all church leaders in every culture need to love and fear a holy God, need to intercede regularly for the people they lead, and need to care deeply for their sinful followers who are created in God's image with infinite worth. Theology and leadership principles are deduced from the text of Scripture.

Just as Scriptural principles lie behind the biblical narrative, so cultural values hide behind the exterior trappings of culture. Some cultural values are overt and open for all to see; other values are submerged at the innermost core of our understanding of life.

While anthropologists have suggested many levels of culture, we will concentrate on three: *worldview,* internal *values* and external *practices.* All three levels are interdependent, strongly influencing each other.[3]

We'll briefly look at the core and the outer layer first. Then we will more thoroughly explore the middle layer of values.

## WORLDVIEW

At the core of culture is *worldview*—beliefs about the deepest meaning of life and assumptions about the nature of reality.[4] All human beings

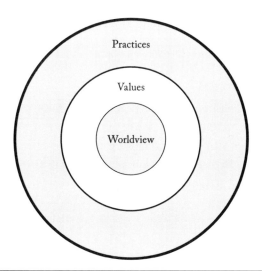

**Figure 4.3**

have ways that they make sense of the world. Is the purpose of life to acquire individual wealth or fame? Is it to promote the reputation of the extended family? Is it to please God? Is it to be happy? Is it to live a sacrificial life for others?

What about the nature of reality? Is there a God, and if so, does he know me and care about me? Is there a heaven and hell? Does the physical world really exist, and if so, is it orderly? Are people good or bad? Do people have free will, or is life controlled by the environment? Do evil spirits and angels exist? Is there such a thing as absolute truth? These philosophical and theological presuppositions subtly direct all other cultural values that influence the practice of leadership. People are aware of some aspects of their worldview, but most assumptions are implicit.

## CULTURAL PRACTICES

Clothing fashions, food preferences, wedding traditions, musical styles, farming techniques and family traditions are a few of the millions of external practices that are influenced by culture. Cultural differences in external preferences are pretty obvious. In the food category, we've savored spicy curry in India, *kimchi* in Korea, and *injira ba wat* in Ethiopia. We've delighted in the variety of musical styles used to praise God around the world—from the minor melodies and syncopated rhythms of Latin America to the staid, pure choir music in Korea.

External practices are easy to spot, but we seldom think about the underlying worldview they convey. What is the connection between *worldview* and *practices*?

Let's imagine we live in a country where the worldview assumes that self-actualization of the individual is the highest purpose of life. How might the external values in this culture reflect this deep-seated worldview? We might observe that people spend most of their time by themselves, working in private offices or cubicles. Even in a crowd, people listen to music through personal earphones. On busy sidewalks people do not stop to greet each other or even make eye contact. People drive alone in their cars. Parents and teachers give children freedom, wanting them to be innovative and self-confident. Schools encourage creativity, avoiding competition, standardized testing or grades that could hurt the feelings of the child. At home children have separate bedrooms. Politicians in this interesting country seek to promote individual freedom within limited government. Psychologists are not directive, but desire to be good listeners to help people overcome inferiority complexes. Teens who break the law are not called criminals. Instead, they are described as "youth who have self-esteem problems." We could go on and on.

While this make-believe country may sound a bit far-fetched (or all too familiar), it illustrates the connection between the foundational worldview and the pervasive external preferences of a culture. The actualization of the individual drives the visible preferences.

## CULTURAL VALUES

The *worldview* of a culture describes deep philosophical assumptions about the purpose of life and the nature of reality. Cultural *practices* are the externals, the things we can see, hear, smell, taste or touch: architecture, music, food, clothing, language, transportation and hair style. But in between are *values,* cultural ideals that link abstract philosophy to concrete practices. For instance, if the *worldview* of a culture is materialism, we might observe the *practice* of people in a hurry, doing a lot of things to make money. Tying together worldview and practice we could hypothesize inner *values* of efficiency, time as money, and business goals trumping personal relationships. A culture where people *practice* meditation may reflect a *worldview* of existential mysticism, reflecting *values* of internal harmony.

Cultural values relating to leadership are subconscious assumptions about how people think about power, handle ambiguity, prize individualism, achieve status or plan for the future. In the next several chapters we will investigate ways that internal values impact leadership in the global church.

From my experience, the greatest difficulties in multicultural leadership arise from tensions growing out of internal values. These values are assumed, hidden, subtle and unspoken. Internal values about leadership cause so many misunderstandings because they are below the surface. Most of us don't think about them. We often assume that everyone has similar values and are surprised when differences become the cause of mix-ups and tensions.

It is dangerous, though, to overemphasize cultural differences. In the deepest sense, human beings are more alike than different. Physically we have similar DNA, blood type, bone structure, facial features and thousands of other characteristics. Socially we have similar needs for belonging, acceptance, security and fulfillment. Cognitively our differences are variations on a limited number of themes. Spiritually we are formed in the image of God, with the special breath of God. We have the ability to know and love God. The paradox is that all human beings are mostly alike, yet each is distinct.

Three things that shape us are our common human nature, the culture that fashioned us, and individual personalities that make us unique. Most likely the four ancient temperaments—sanguine, choleric, phlegmatic and melancholic—can be found in every culture.[5] Anthropologists observe that personality "is the outcome of a lifelong process of interaction between an organism and its ecocultural and sociocultural environment. The effects of these external factors make it likely that there are systematic differences in the person—typical behavior of people who have been brought up in different cultures."[6]

## CULTURE MATTERS

Some critics argue that with the end of the Cold War, growing globalization, instant communication and economic development, cultural differences are no longer crucial. When short-term missionaries return from travels to distant cultures, they often exclaim, "Those people are just like us!" Yes, the world seems to be getting smaller. Carol and I were waiting for our luggage at the Abuja airport in Nigeria and were surprised to hear the voice of Jimmy Reeves singing "Just a Closer Walk with Thee." At the airport in La Paz, Bolivia, we smiled as the Gypsy Kings sang in Spanish "A Mi Manera" ("I Did It My Way"). Globalization has spread many common traditions, but as it gains momentum, so does the influence of local cultural values.

Samuel P. Huntington, in his somewhat controversial book, *The Clash of Civilizations*, seeks to dispel the myth that the world is becoming homogeneous and that culture no longer makes a difference.

In the post–Cold War world, the most important distinctions among peoples are not ideological, political or economic. They are cultural. People and nations are attempting to answer the most basic question humans can face: Who are we? And they are answering that question in the traditional way human beings have answered it, by reference to the things that mean the most to them. People define themselves in terms of ancestry, religion, language, history, values, customs and institutions.[7]

Thomas Friedman makes an impressive case both for the growing impact of globalization as well as the enduring influence of local culture. He uses the metaphor of the Lexus and the olive tree.

Olive trees are important. They represent everything that roots us, anchors us, identifies us and locates us in this world—whether it be belonging to a family, a community, a tribe, a nation, a religion or, most of all, a place called home. . . . We fight so intensely at times over our olive trees because, at their best, they provide the feelings of self-esteem and belonging that are as essential for human survival as food in the belly.

So what does the Lexus represent? It represents an equally fundamental, age-old human drive—the drive for sustenance, improvement, prosperity and modernization—as it is played out in today's globalization system.[8]

While the externals of clothing, food, music, transportation and the Internet are changing and making the world more homogeneous, deep cultural values seem to be ever more stable and enduring. Globalization might make us look more alike on the outside, but localization reinforces the deepest inner being of our identities.

How does this double effect of globalization and the strengthening of local culture relate to leadership in the worldwide church? The more we interact with each other, the more we need to understand each other's underlying cultural values. The more churches in the West and Asia partner with churches in Africa and Latin America, the more deeply we need to be aware of how culture permeates hidden assumptions about leadership. External similarities in global leadership can lull us into complacency. We may think we understand leaders in other cultures when in fact our ignorance can cause serious misunderstandings. Globalization means that people are looking more and more alike on the outside, but the inner layer of cultural values hasn't changed very much.

Culture influences every facet of our lives. Edward T. Hall writes:

> There is not one aspect of human life that is not touched and altered by culture. This means personality, how people express themselves (including shows of emotion), the way they think, how they move, how problems are solved, how their cities are planned and laid out, how transportation systems function and are organized, as well as how economic and government systems are put together and function.[9]

Since the effects of culture are so pervasive, they powerfully influence the way leaders solve problems, delegate authority, set goals, organize churches and plan mission trips. As churches gain a global perspective and missionaries are sent from everywhere to everywhere, it makes sense to pay special attention to the impact of culture on leadership.

To work in harmony, leaders in the global church must recognize and appreciate cultural differences in both external preferences and internal values. The following chapters will examine these values in depth.

# REFLECTIONS ON MULTICULTURAL LEADERSHIP

Dr. David Bremner, Deputy International Director for SIM, with responsibility for Eastern and Southern Africa

As I worked in pioneer church planting and leadership development in rural Paraguay, I often pondered the source of the many different leadership styles that I have been privileged to observe. I worked first as part of a team of Western missionaries, and then in a leadership team made up of a variety of nationalities. My wife, Nikki, and I are from South Africa. We have lived most of our adult lives in Paraguay and are now based in the United States, where we work in international mission administration.

At the deepest level one's worldview clearly plays a role in how leadership is viewed. Personality types also greatly influence one's approach to social interaction in leadership. Personal experiences, observation and training probably play the most conscious role in developing one's leadership style. Far less recognizable than these is the conditioning that culture and language have on the leader-follower dynamics of leadership.

As I have observed and interviewed church leaders in Paraguay I am more than ever convinced that their understanding of church leadership has more to do with cultural norms than with biblical instruction. As I became aware of this I began to ponder the leadership styles (and literature) of the Western churches. It would appear to me that church leadership in the West is as conditioned by culture as it is in Paraguay. A lot of the current popular literature on Christian leadership tracks closely with the current cultural leadership practices and literature. We have become so adept at matching biblical passages with cultural leadership patterns that one wonders if what is portrayed as biblical leadership is not merely Christian spice added to cultural broths.

The Paraguayan concept of leadership comes from nomadic family groups, Christianized by the *"conquistadores"* and politically freed by powerful *"libertadores."* The strong-man (or *caudillo*) leadership style is expected by everyone. The Catholic church in Paraguay has no problem fitting in and perpetuating this leadership style with the authority of the priesthood and vows of obedience. The evangelical churches have adopted church government structures brought by missionaries from different Western-based denominations. Church leaders have managed to fit into these governance structures, but have done so in a "spiritualized" strongman fashion. One pastor told me that no one can be a member or leader in his church without 100 percent allegiance, obedience and loyalty to his person. The biblical basis for this, according to him, is Ephesians 4:11 ("It was he who gave some to be apostles, some to be prophets, some to be evangelists, and some to be pastors and teachers" NIV). Since it is God himself who "gave some to be . . . pastors," he believes he has God's authority in the church.

Similarly, the concept of the parish priest has been practiced in Western evangelical churches for centuries in the form of the professional pastoral couple. Smaller churches have one pastoral couple. More staff members are added as the church grows. Large churches operate in the pattern of the CEO-led board. This pattern for leadership appears to come from the current cultural leadership system. We need to ask whether this leads to genuine contextualization of biblical leadership or if Christian people are merely practicing culturally conditioned leadership in the context of the church.

# LEADERSHIP AND CONTEXT

*Beneath the clearly perceived, highly explicit surface culture,*
*there lies a whole other world.*

EDWARD HALL, *BEYOND CULTURE*

MY CANADIAN COLLEAGUE HOWARD BRANT TELLS about a meeting
with a group of Asian church leaders who were trying to select a director for their mission organization. They talked for awhile about the
position and the desired characteristics of the leader. One person in the
group was identified as a potential leader. Howard asked the group if
they would support this person. Each person answered one by one,
"yes," "yes," "yes." When they came to the man in question at the end of
the line, he said, "See—they really don't want me." Howard said, "It
was then I realized that there were discreet cultural signals understood
between them which I had totally missed!" He learned that what you
see or hear is not necessarily what you get. In some mysterious way the
men were subtly saying, "No, we don't want this man as the director."
The explicit message was one of agreement, but the subtle context sig-
naled something else.

Edward T. Hall sheds light on the situation: "Beneath the clearly
perceived, highly explicit surface culture, there lies a whole other world,
which when understood will ultimately radically change our view of
human nature."[1]

Probably the most fundamental difference between people and cultures is the degree of sensitivity to what is happening around them—their context. Some cultures encourage people to tune in closely to innuendoes of meaning occurring all around them, subtle though these may be. Other cultures predispose people to be divorced from their physical context and more deeply connected to the world of ideas. Once I began to understand the significance of how people interact with their context, hundreds of confusing experiences began to make sense. It was as if I had discovered a submerged iceberg for understanding the fundamentals of culture. As Hall writes, "Like the invisible jet streams in the skies that determine the course of a storm, these hidden currents shape our lives; yet their influence is only beginning to be identified."[2]

The profound significance of context hit me as I read Hall's book *Beyond Culture*.

> A high-context (HC) communication or message is one in which most of the information is either in the physical context or internalized in the person, while very little is in the coded, explicit, transmitted part of the message. A low-context (LC) communication is just the opposite; i.e., the mass of the information is vested in the explicit code. Twins who have grown up together can and do communicate more economically (HC) than two lawyers in a courtroom during a trial (LC).[3]

*A high-context culture* is made up of people who pay special attention to the concrete world around them. Everything in the physical setting communicates something significant: the atmosphere of the room, the sounds, the smells, the expressions on faces, the body language. The subtleties of the real-life setting intentionally communicate important information. Hall gives examples of high-context cultures from Africa, Asia, South America and the Middle East.

In *low-context cultures,* people pay special attention to explicit communication and to ideas. The context of these ideas is not as important as what is specifically said. Precise words are more important than the tone of voice. The flowery language common in a high-context culture will sound insincere or even deceitful to a low-context person. The big idea of an important conversation may be remembered, but not the name of the person involved in the discussion. While people in high-context cultures are deeply embedded in the immediate world around them, low-context people are immersed in the world of concepts, principles and ideas. One is high context, the other high idea.

Howard Brant's illustration of the leadership discussions in Asia is a powerful example of the significance of context in communication. From Howard's low-context perspective each committee member had agreed to the leadership selection, but everyone in the high-context situation knew that the real vote was unanimous disagreement. Unspoken cues were obvious to the insiders and were more influential than the spoken words.

High-context cultures place a premium on harmonious relationships. The group is more valued than the individual, and cooperation is preferred over competition. Quality time is treasured more than accomplishing a quantitative task. Change is often resisted.

On the other hand, people in low-context cultures tend to think in concepts, principles, abstractions and theories. Their thinking transcends the present situation and is not embedded in the immediate context. Communication is not subtle, but direct. It is mostly verbal or written. Accomplishing precise goals is more important than building relationships, and time is measured as a quantity, not a quality. Because communication is unambiguous, the meaning can be understood by outsiders as well as insiders.[4] Individuality and competition are valued, and change is usually seen as a good thing.

Tension and confusion between cultures arises in the hidden messages enfolded in the context. Low-context communication can seem cold and uncaring to people in high-context cultures, and high-context communication can seem baffling or even dishonest to idea-oriented people.[5]

I once met an American missionary couple in West Africa who were being sent home by local pastors. Tension festered for many months until the pastors asked the couple to leave the country. The missionary couple was crushed. They had spent two hard years raising finances and two more years to learn the local language. Having given up high-paying business careers, they endured homesickness and malaria. They thought they had been sensitive to the culture and had worked to make many friends. Now they were being asked to go home. The wife blurted out, "Why didn't you tell us that we were offending you? We would have been more than willing to change!" The local pastor responded that many people had been telling them about the problem for months, but they just didn't listen.

The couple was sure that the local pastors were being dishonest, and the local pastors were sure that the missionaries were insensitive to what they assumed was clear communication. The Americans might have subtly demonstrated condescending attitudes, and the African pastors might have communicated discreetly by tone of voice or by what they didn't say. On both sides a lack of understanding about the importance of context caused much sorrow.

Although understanding cultural values related to context is helpful, in reality people don't fit neatly into simple categories. For instance, it's too simplistic to assume that Europeans are low context and Africans are high context. Because of unique personalities, a range of values is present in each culture. Children within the same family may have very different values and temperaments regarding time or goals, and people are also capable of changing their cultural values—"shifting gears" depending on the situation. An efficiency-oriented lawyer might become laid-back on vacation and be quite content to wait for fish to bite. But most people operate using preferred values with which they feel comfortable most of the time.

While it is important to avoid stereotypes, the research of Edward T. Hall indicates that cultures tend to favor one or the other contextual value. Connerly and Pedersen affirm this tendency:

> In high-context cultures, such as China, Korea, Japan, France, Greece, and many Arab countries, what is unsaid but understood carries more weight that what is actually written down or said. . . . In low-context cultures, such as the American, Scandinavian, German, and Swiss, the focus is on the specifics of what is written or said, and trust is gained through legal agreements. Handshakes, while often given, are not sufficient to establish a contractual agreement, and personal relationships detract from business.[6]

Strengths and weaknesses characterize both low- and high-context perspectives. For instance, special awareness of nonverbal communication may be a strength of a high-context culture. Leaders from a low-context culture may need to be nudged toward this awareness. By the same token, leaders from high-context cultures might benefit from planning strategies that are a strength of low-context cultures. Both sides need to be patient with each other.

While all cultures fall on a continuum of both perspectives, each leans toward valuing either events or ideas. Families, churches and organizations also reflect a preference toward high or low context.

## CONTEXT AND COMMUNICATION

I've asked a variety of leaders working in multicultural teams to describe their greatest delights and struggles. Many pinpoint direct and indirect communication as their greatest frustration. Essentially, this is the challenge of understanding low-context and high-context cultures.

One veteran missionary tells about working under a gifted and articulate African pastor. A number of interns also worked under this pastor, but within six months, conflict between the pastor and the interns would inevitably erupt. The pattern of losing good interns was disturbing, and the missionary raised the issue at a church board meeting. That board meeting fractured the relationship the missionary had with the pastor. In effect, he had challenged the pastor publicly, causing him to lose face. In retrospect, he wishes he had spoken privately with the pastor rather than addressing the issue in a public setting. This would have helped to preserve honor (versus causing shame)—one of the most important cultural values in a high-context society. It would also have preserved their relationship. Direct communication seems to be the proper way of handling conflict in a low-context culture, but it can bring shame in a high-context culture.

Low-context cultures tend to speak truth directly rather than seeking to protect relationships. In high-context cultures, truth is spoken in much more subtle forms, seeking above all to preserve relationships. Often an advocate or intermediary is used instead of dealing directly one-on-one. This tends to soften the interaction in a way that protects relationships.

Reverend Oscar Muriu is pastor of the Nairobi Chapel, a church with thousands of members and dozens of church plants. In an interview published in *Christianity Today*, he describes how communication takes place in Africa.

> When we communicate in Africa, we are very guarded in what we say. We don't want to offend. Westerners say that Africans never tell you what they really think. They tell you what you want to hear. And yes, that's true! Because from our perspective, every engagement between two people always has the potential of leading to a lifelong relationship, or preventing a lifelong friendship.
>
> Africa is a very relational continent. It's the relationships that make society work.
>
> In the U.S. things work irrespective of relationships; in fact, if you have a relationship, it can sometimes work against you. In Africa it's the opposite. So we are always guarded and gracious in our communication. We want to guard the relationship. When the Bible says, "Speak the truth in love," we err on the side of love. The possibility of a relationship means I cannot tell you the total truth until I am secure in this relationship with you, until I know that the truth will not hurt this relationship.
>
> You do it differently. Speaking the truth has a higher premium in your context, so you are unguarded. You speak the truth, call a spade a spade, at whatever cost. And if the relationship suffers, well, that's too bad, the important thing is that the truth was spoken.
>
> We never do that. I've had to learn to be more assertive in my dealings with Americans just so they would hear me! I have had to learn to speak truth more directly. Americans have to learn to listen to the relational side of things.[7]

In a high-context culture, it is often preferable to delay a decision rather than to agree on what is seen as unwelcome news. It may be quite obvious that a policy needs to change, but if this policy has the potential to cause disruption, no firm decision will be communicated. "We are still studying the matter" is one response that frustrates leaders who are accustomed to efficient decision-making in low-context cultures. They would prefer to tell the bad news and get it over with, while high-context leaders prefer not to disappoint people, telling them to wait instead.

People in every culture are capable of communicating, thinking and leading in many different ways, but most cultures have a preference toward low or high context.

## CONTEXT AND TIME

During our missionary service in Nigeria I was assigned to set up a multimedia department. Lacking funds, we earned money for the department by taking photographs for Nigerian businesses. Our first assignment was to shoot calendar pictures for a large textile mill in Kaduna.

As I drove into the huge complex, the guard at the gate escorted me straight to the head office of the chief executive officer of the company. I assumed this was a mistake and that the CEO would redirect me to someone lower on the organization chart. But no, I was in the right place. He sat me down in his office, offered me a Coke and asked about my trip. Within thirty seconds the phone rang with the message that a cotton truck had broken down in the entrance road and was blocking other trucks. He quickly gave orders to the guard and continued with my interview. In less than a minute we were again interrupted as a boy barged into the office with a case of Coke, asking where it should go. The CEO directed him to another office where they were short. As he again explained the format of the photos he needed, another manager burst in with a problem concerning one of the weaving machines.

Our conversation lasted for nearly an hour, with dozens of disruptions. It struck me that everyone in the whole corporation reported directly to the CEO. No one made appointments and there seemed to be no chain of command. At first I was bothered by the distractions, but as we continued, my frustration turned to great admiration. I was amazed that one man knew so much about such a complex operation and that he could carry on a half dozen logical conversations at the same time.

An understanding of culture and context helps us understand this interesting phenomenon. Edward T. Hall proposes a relationship between the ways high- and low-context cultures think of time. He observes that high-context cultures are polychronic, while low-context cultures are monochronic. In polychronic cultures several things happen at the same time, while people in monochronic cultures tend to do one thing at a time.[8] Hall suggests that North American and Northern European people tend to view time as monochronic, valuing schedules, segmentation and promptness.[9] Polychronic systems found in Asia, Latin America, the Middle East and Africa "are characterized by several things happening at once. They stress involvement of people and completing of transactions rather than adherence to preset schedules."[10]

Space is related to time. It is difficult to do one thing at a time if one can be constantly interrupted. Office space in monochronic cultures isolates people behind tall, sound-deadening cubicles or closed-door offices. Polychronic offices are often large rooms where everyone is able to see everyone else.

During our years in Nigeria I reported to a polychronic superior. The reason I could never get an appointment was because I assumed that if someone was in his office during my appointment time, I should not interrupt. I also assumed that if I had official business with him that I needed to conduct it in his office during office hours, and not in his living room in the evening. I eventually learned to stick my head in his office with my question even if he had visitors, and increasingly felt at ease doing business in his home.

When I directed the Department of Theological Education for the denomination, I was constantly interrupted by school principals, teachers, students and other missionaries. It was impossible for my secretary to tell unexpected visitors that I was alone in my office yet was not able to see them. While I enjoyed the unpredictability of the daily schedule, at times I needed to be alone to work on a project. Rather than turn people away, I cleaned up an old chicken coop behind our house, put screens on the windows and added a light bulb and a desk. No one seemed offended if I was out of the office. Because I could "hide" in my monochronic office when a deadline loomed, I felt at ease in my official polychronic office and visited with whomever happened to drop by.

Polychronic, high-context cultures value interactions with people and events. Time is not divided into predetermined appointments, and space is not segmented into offices and living rooms. Low-context cultures are monochronic. Business is conducted at a precise time and location, while interactions with family and friends take place in a different time and place.

## CONTEXT AND THE CHURCH

We attend a Presbyterian church that leans toward the low-context end of the spectrum. The choir and musical instruments perform behind the congregation in the balcony so that facial expressions and body movements will not overpower the message. Such an arrangement would seem strange to a high-context congregation. Recently one of our Hispanic friends visited our church. She commented that the pastor had good things to say, but she preferred a preacher who spoke with more enthusiasm and passion.

Another couple visited our church for only one Sunday. When I asked why they chose to attend a different church they answered, "Your people don't really pray or worship. No one raised their hands or clapped." I suspect that if some of our church members attended this couple's church they would object to the emotionalism, preferring more serious and reverent worship. Personally, I feel at home in our church and appreciate the dignity and thoughtfulness of the service, but I understand that our approach can seem cold and formal to high-context worshipers.

Contrast the above low-context church with the high-context church we attended in Nigeria. The church service began when most of the people arrived, usually about thirty to forty-five minutes after the stated time. We didn't have bulletins because the order of activities changed several times depending on how many special numbers were available and how many visitors wanted to give greetings. Not having a bulletin meant we could be flexible to the leading of the Spirit. Members of the Women's Fellowship choir carried babies on their backs and wore wrappers made of matching cloth. They swayed together, accompanied by traditional percussion instruments. Instead of ushers quietly taking up the offering, everyone "danced" up the aisle to put money in an offering box. If not enough money came in the first offering, the pastor would call for a second one. The walls of the church were plastered with banners, calendars and posters. Christmas lights remained over the pulpit long after Christmas. The preacher expounded on a topic with great emotion and vivid illustrations. The service ended when everything was finished—not at a set time. Everything in the environment was part of the experience. The service flowed out of the values of a high-context culture, and we thoroughly enjoyed it.

Cultural values are so critical that low-context churches may not be able to attract high-context people and vice versa. More churches seem to be splitting over music style than theology. Critics of contemporary Christian music complain that it is filled with meaningless repetition and lacks the thoughtful theology of the old hymns of the faith. Proponents of contemporary music make the case that the music fits the culture of today's youth. Dr. Johann Buis, a South African musicologist, comments about the debate over contemporary Christian music:

> The whole argument in "the worship wars" is totally misplaced. . . . The body in motion, repetition, emotion-laden expression—these key components to [contemporary Christian music] are part of a framework that comes out of Africa. . . . They stand in contrast to the nonemotive, linear forms of music that come out of the European Enlightenment. People have generated so much anger on the level of preference—but the real issues are not theological, but cultural.[11]

Table 5.1 represents worship services at extreme ends of a continuum, but illustrates how internal cultural values of high- and low-context perspectives influence external cultural preferences in worship and preaching. Most churches are a mixture of high- and low-context orientation.

People from high- and low-context cultures can learn valuable perspectives from each other. The beauty of crosscultural intermingling is that differences enrich our experience of God's grace.

The danger of a service that is overly high-context is that it can lead to shallow emotionalism, self-centeredness and false teaching, while the danger of overly idea-oriented worship is that it can lead to dead orthodoxy. Paul reminded the church in Corinth to pray and sing with the spirit and with understanding (1 Cor 14:15). Apparently the temptation of the early church was to dichotomize between a high-context emotionalism without understanding or a low-context worship without passion.

**Table 5.1. High-Context and Low-Context Churches**

|  | High-Context Churches | Low-Context Churches |
|---|---|---|
| **Sermon** | Topical sermons, drawing on the Bible, but emphasizing meeting the present needs of the people | Expository sermons, concentrating on what the Bible says and less on the immediate felt needs of the people |
| **Preaching Style** | Friendly tone of voice and hand motions; preacher walks among the people | Dignity and linear logic; preacher stands behind the pulpit and often reads the sermon |
| **Music Style** | Vigorous music with raised hands and body movement, often singing about "what God means to me" | Quiet, thoughtful singing about the attributes of God; emphasis on reverence |
| **Seating** | Seating so people can see each other | Seats facing the preacher |
| **Order of Service** | As the Lord leads | Follows the printed bulletin |
| **Length of Service** | As long as it takes | Precisely set time |
| **Prayer** | With emotion and loud Amens, sometimes all praying at the same time | Leader reads a prayer with quiet thoughtfulness |
| **Ambiance** | Banners, video clips, data projector, informal, coffee in the sanctuary | Plain, so as not to detract from the message |

My hunch is that the Lord made some individuals and cultures with a preference for standing still while they sing and pray in church. He made others who prefer to move with outstretched arms in praise and prayer. God delights in variations of his creation, and I doubt he intended us to criticize each other for our worship styles.

## CONTEXT AND LEADERSHIP

Most leadership practices can be traced back to the foundational concepts of high- versus low-context lenses for seeing the world.

Let's look again at the dilemma between Hans and Pastor Luka in Togo (chap. 4). Both have different *internal values* regarding planning, interpersonal relationships and status. Hans operates from a low-context orientation, and Luka is deeply influenced by the high-context current situation. Hans would like to plan with a twelve-month flow chart, estimating abstract variables such as time and resources. Luka is oriented toward the present urgent need of ministering to people dying

Table 5.2. High-Context and Low-Context Leadership[a]

|  | High-Context Leadership | Low-Context Leadership |
| --- | --- | --- |
| Time | Many things can happen at the same time. It may be difficult to begin and end a meeting on time, or to isolate one activity at a time. | Meetings begin and end on time and should be scheduled in an orderly sequence. People want to stick to the agenda. |
| Communication Style | Communication is indirect, with emphasis on nonverbal messages. Tone of voice, posture and facial features have group meaning. | Communication is direct—either spoken or written. The idea being discussed is more important than the feelings behind the statement. |
| Authority | Prestige is given by the group and becomes almost permanent. Others will be expected to respect rank. Formal credentials are important and need to be evident. Age is often a criteria for respect. | Authority is earned by individual effort and accomplishment. It is temporary and dependent on continued successful performance. Formal credentials are not as important as performance. |
| Leadership Style | Leadership is usually controlling in order to maintain group harmony and conformity. The leader often has a charismatic personality. Leaders reward loyalty. Followers appreciate strong leaders. | Leaders allow others to have significant input into decision making. Followers are more likely to question the ideas and decisions of the leader. Leaders respect individual initiative from group members. |
| Conflict Resolution Style | Indirect resolution is sought through mutual friends. Displeasure is shown through nonverbal, subtle communication. Direct conflict resolution may be avoided for as long as possible. Preserving harmony is emphasized. | Resolution is sought through direct confrontation. People will meet face to face and articulate difficulties verbally. Speaking the truth is emphasized and appreciated. |
| Goals | The highest goal is to build interpersonal relationships and make friends. Group harmony is highly valued. | Goals are task-oriented. The leader will want to accomplish a precise, predetermined job within a prescribed time frame. |

of AIDS and would like to begin as soon as possible. Luka would like to appoint a director he knows and trusts. Hans is more interested in finding someone with professional experience and is concerned about the pitfalls of nepotism. Again we see the clash between high and low context—between a known personal relationship and the abstract idea of proper credentials. Luka realizes that local people will have greater respect for the director if he drives an expensive car, and this will add credibility for the whole project. Hans is concerned about tax laws and the efficient use of funds.

Pastor Luka and Hans need each other! Both have perspectives that can help those who suffer from AIDS. They need to take the time to build mutual understanding and appreciation of each other's orientation toward events and ideas. If they don't, the project will likely fall apart. Luka and Hans need to realize that both of their perspectives have strengths and weaknesses.

Hans could become so enamored with low-context abstract planning that he ignores the AIDS victims, and high-context Luka could become so passionate about the AIDS emergency that, in the long run, the ministry is hindered for lack of sound planning. Hans needs to understand the importance of credibility in the eyes of the local people, and Luka needs to appreciate the need for experienced leadership and the limitations of funds. If the two can work together, the different values will complement each other to build a stronger and more effective AIDS ministry.

Bringing to full light the leadership values of one's own culture is the first step toward mutual effectiveness. Hans and Pastor Luka also need to investigate Scripture together. Where clear biblical principles contradict cultural values, the Bible takes precedence, but where the Bible leaves room for flexibility, the cultural values of the local host culture should normally prevail. Other times, the local culture should benefit from leadership insights brought by those of other cultures.

# REFLECTIONS ON
# MULTICULTURAL LEADERSHIP

Alfredo Umaña, Honduras

"Yes, they are different!" our pastor exclaimed on the day of our wedding.

Being married to my beloved American wife has been both a challenge and a joy. It has required me to lead using the three words our minister challenged us to practice as a couple. These are also key words for leading crossculturally in any context.

*Forbear.* The different speed of our decision-making processes has tested our patience. Lisa will be acting while I am still pondering. I still remember the day we went to Best Buy, and before I realized it, we were going out of the store with stereo equipment. Once we were in the car, Lisa asked me why I looked so sad. That is when we figured it out—I did not agree with the purchase, but I did not express it in time. One hour later we were in the return line. Over the years I have gotten better at thinking and acting—and Lisa has gotten better at waiting and learning.

*Forsake.* I thought that renouncing my Honduran food was going to be my biggest challenge in my crosscultural marriage, but I have found that relinquishing the image of the husband as the one who decides and the wife who submits has been more difficult than not eating *tortillas* every day. Learning to lead by consensus has been a valuable lesson. Learning to give my wife freedom to act with the certainty that I will intervene if she needs guidance or correction has been a challenge. One example of this kind of leadership has been my input in helping her to deal with relationships in Latin America. It is very common now that Lisa will invite me to read a letter or an email that she is sending to check if it is culturally appropriate. I have forsaken authoritarianism and she has forsaken independence.

*Forgive.* This is definitely the winner! I have had to forgive her confrontational style in solving conflicts and she has had to forgive my passive aggressiveness. Communication has been the key. I will surely affirm that leading crossculturally needs more intentional communication than leading people of your own culture. One of the most useful questions has been, What did you really mean when you said so and so?

I often caution Lisa not to get overcommitted, yet she still does. When she discovers she is in over her head she complains that I was not emphatic enough in stopping her. But in reality, Latins' communication style is indirect, relying heavily on nonverbal and indirect cues. That's when I have to forgive her for not "listening" to me. She prefers direct, precise, to-the-point, explicit communication, so she has to forgive me for not being "direct" enough.

Three crosscultural leadership keys: Forbear, Forsake, Forgive.

# LEADERSHIP AND POWER

*Don't ever let anyone call you "Rabbi," for you have only one teacher,*
*and all of you are on the same level as brothers and sisters.*

JESUS, MATTHEW 23:8 NLT

DURING A TRIP TO KOREA, I WAS ASKED to speak at a large church
several hours south of Seoul. As I stepped off the train I was greeted
warmly by a dignified delegation of the pastor and two elders, who
then proceeded to ask if I was ordained. I lightheartedly quoted Scripture, saying that I was "foreordained before the foundation of the earth."
I also said I was an ordained elder in our church. I could hear them
talking quietly with each other in Korean. I found out later that since I
was not an ordained pastor, my translator would need to be ordained. If
I had been ordained, anyone could translate for me. Even though I had
a Ph.D. and was the head of a major international mission agency, the
fact that I was not ordained caused a problem for them. It was an awk-
ward moment. I sensed, though, that their consternation made sense in
a culture with high-power-distance values. These church leaders understood cultural expectations and wanted to give me as much credibility as possible in the eyes of their congregation. My academic credentials were appreciated, but ordination was esteemed as the highest
credential and essential for preaching.

In every society certain people have more power, influence and status than others, and each society develops cultural values that deal with inequality. Some cultures assume a large status gap between those who have power and those who don't. In these cultures, both leaders and followers assume that the power gap is natural and good. These societies are called *high-power-distance* cultures. Other cultures value lesser power distance and seek to minimize status symbols and inequalities between people. These are called *low-power-distance* cultures. All cultures fit along a power-distance continuum.

## SOCIAL SCIENCE RESEARCH AND LEADERSHIP

The Bible sheds valuable light on the nature of people, but God has also given us minds and a sense of curiosity to discover more understanding from general revelation. Hundreds of excellent research studies give insights on how God made people and how leaders in the global church can work in harmony across cultures.

Numerous people have written and researched the topic of leadership. The best summary of research on leadership is by Bernard and Ruth Bass.[1] The fourth edition of *The Bass Handbook of Leadership*, published in 2008, of 1,500 pages, summarizes thousands of research studies in leadership and includes chapters on globalization, cross-national effects, and minorities as leaders and followers. Their bibliography includes over 8,000 references and stretches to 218 pages of double-column, small-print entries. I have constantly referred to this book in my writing.

For our purposes we will look at three major leadership studies, one in each of the next three chapters. All three have a large sample size from multiple countries to compare leadership variables among cultures. While most smaller studies investigate two or three variables between two or three countries, these three studies look at dozens of leadership values from scores of countries.

The most well-known study is by Geert Hofstede, a researcher from the Netherlands.[2] He studied IBM employees from 74 countries with over 100,000 people in his sample. The first edition of his book *Cultures and Organizations: Software of the Mind*, has been translated into seventeen languages.

Another major study is *Riding the Waves of Culture: Understanding Cultural Diversity in Business,* by Fons Trompenaars and Charles Hampden-Turner.[3] This study included 30,000 participants from 31 countries, investigating how people in different parts of the world understand such leadership qualities as rules, groups, feelings, status and time.

A third study, the most sophisticated, is by Robert J. House and others, *Culture, Leadership and Organizations: The GLOBE Study of 62 Societies.*[4] GLOBE stands for Global Leadership and Organizational Behavior Effectiveness. This project may be the most comprehensive of all the studies so far. One hundred and seventy researchers worked on the project, costing millions of dollars. They tested 27 hypotheses with a sample size of 17,300 managers.[5] Their research confirmed many of the concepts from Hofstede, and also added new dimensions to his study.

There is no such thing as perfect research. No matter how carefully researchers work to produce a reliable study, rival hypotheses will always emerge. Hofstede has been criticized for the inability of researchers to replicate some of his variables with a different sample.[6] The GLOBE study has been challenged by Harry Triandis, questioning whether large countries like India, China or the United States can be represented by a single sample. Triandis also questions if the translation of the word *leadership* into different cultures has the same meaning. For example, in Greece the term *archon* has connotations from the root word *archondas,* "a rather arrogant upper class person."[7] Nevertheless, well-designed research sheds valuable insights into the nature of people, culture and leadership.

Understanding cultural values doesn't solve the dilemma of whether we should follow or confront expectations, but it fosters in us a more positive attitude about the motives of people who misunderstand us.

## RESEARCH ON POWER DISTANCE

The GLOBE study defines power distance as "the degree to which members of an organization expect and agree that power should be shared unequally."[8] Hofstede defines power distance as "the extent to which the less powerful members of institutions and organizations within a country expect and accept that power is distributed unequally."[9]

In high-power-distance cultures both leaders and followers assume that the leader has more authority, respect and status symbols. The leader has the right to make unilateral decisions that will be obeyed without question. In these societies, employees do not question managers, students do not challenge teachers, and children obey parents or other elders without question. The opposite is true in low-power-distance cultures. Children expect parents to give them a rationale for their decisions. Employees are invited to give suggestions to management, and teachers are glad when students raise difficult questions.

Formal authority tends to be centralized in high-power-distance societies. Bosses are not questioned, and decisions are communicated from the top. For a leader in a high-power-distance culture to ask the advice of a subordinate could signal that the boss doesn't know how to lead.

Leaders in low-power-distance cultures prefer a consultative, participative or democratic decision-making style. Power is delegated to team members or to subcommittees. In very low-power-distance cultures, subordinates would expect to vote on each significant decision.

In high-power-distance cultures, people assume that their leaders will have special privileges such as their own parking space, a corner office, finer clothes, a private dining room, a much higher salary and maybe a chauffeured car. None of this will be expected of leaders in low-power-distance cultures and, in fact, would irritate employees.

## POWER DISTANCE BY COUNTRY

While generalizations oversimplify, the research by Hofstede shows that in general Asian, Eastern European, African and several Latin American countries recorded relatively high-power-distance values. Northern Europe, along with Great Britain, the United States, Israel, New Zealand, Australia and some Latin American countries tend toward low-power-distance values.[10] Geographic generalizations can be confusing though. For example in the GLOBE study, Guatemala, Ecuador and Colombia were very strong in the practice of high power distance, but Costa Rica and Bolivia ranked near the bottom. Nigeria,

Zimbabwe and Zambia appeared very high in the practice of high power distance, but black South African managers practiced a low level of power distance. India and South Korea scored very high in power distance, while Japan, China and Singapore measured moderately high.[11]

Even though the data showing differences between countries is interesting and statistically significant, it is good to be suspicious of generalizations. India and China are home to over a billion people each, and variations within these countries are probably much greater than the average differences between countries. Social class, level of education, urban/rural demographics and occupation all influence power-distance values. Hofstede found significant differences in Europe, with power distance decreasing as one moves up the ladder from unskilled worker, clerical worker, technician, professional worker to top manager.[12] Country differences give a general idea of what to expect, but crosscultural practitioners would be wise to observe and evaluate each encounter with an open mind.

## RELIGION AND POWER DISTANCE

Why do some cultures value high power distance and others do not? What is the source of these values? While there are several possibilities, both Hofstede and the GLOBE study hypothesize a relationship between power distance and religion, with the assumption that religions with hierarchical structures promote high-power-distance leadership values, or that high-power-distance cultures prefer hierarchical religious organizations.

*Islam* has egalitarian tendencies. An important teaching is that "every person has equal value before Allah."[13] There is no chain of command between mosques, and no worldwide hierarchy of leadership. During the pilgrimage to Mecca, all people dress alike and go through the same steps of the journey. But many Muslims hold to a perspective that combines inner faith with the outward institutions of government and law, and this usually results in higher power distance. The GLOBE study also notes that Islam was nurtured in countries that "tended historically to be highly hierarchical in nature."[14] Thus it is not surprising that Morocco, Turkey, Iran, Kazakhstan, Indonesia, Malaysia, Kuwait and Egypt are relatively high in power distance.[15] But Qatar is relatively low on the power-distance scale.

*Hinduism* holds to teachings that could support either high or low power distance. Each individual soul is divine and is engaged in a struggle for purity. Individual differences are caused by one's *karma* or actions. The caste system, while not mentioned in the *Vedas* (Hindu scriptures) and officially illegal in India, is still a pervasive reality of social life. The caste system seems to have a strong influence on power distance. While India may be changing, both the Hofstede and GLOBE studies found the country to be quite high in power distance.[16]

*Confucianism*, while theoretically not a religion, has powerful social implications. *K'ung fu-tzu*, the master teacher, taught his disciples five hierarchical and reciprocal relationships: ruler-minister, father-son, husband-wife, elder brother–younger brother, and senior friend–junior friend. "The senior person is expected to provide support and encouragement for the lower-status person, whereas the lower-status person is expected to give loyalty and respect to the senior person."[17] The Hofstede study finds China and Singapore to be high in power distance, with South Korea, Hong Kong and Japan medium high.[18] The GLOBE study lists South Korea very high, with Japan, China, Singapore and Hong Kong, medium high.[19] It seems that Confucian values influence the culture of leadership.

*Christianity* seems to have influenced leadership values in two directions. Many would argue that early Christianity valued low-power-distance leadership. Before Christianity became an imperial religion, both leadership and theology were decentralized. Gradually church leadership grew in influence until it held power over heads of state. The growth of hierarchy in the church influenced cultures to become high in power distance. Two tenets of the Reformation were the authority of Scripture over the hierarchy of the church and the priesthood of all believers. In countries influenced by the Reformation, the emphasis on the official church and the priests shifted to the Scripture and the lay believer. These countries—Switzerland, Germany, Great Britain, the United States and Scandinavian countries—are some of the lowest in power distance.[20] Nations less affected by the Reformation—Spain, Portugal and Italy—tend toward high power distance. The cause and effect are not obvious. One wonders if societies with a tendency toward high-power-distance values are most attracted to hierarchical religions, or if hierarchical religions promote the cultural value of high power distance? A case can be made that rulers in China promoted Confucian values in order to avoid social chaos and disintegration.[21] Regardless of which precedes the other, values about power and religion reinforce each other.

## THE CHALLENGE FOR HIGH-POWER-DISTANCE SOCIETIES

High power distance may be seen as paternalism, which carries uncomplimentary connotations for many in countries of northern European heritage. In other parts of the world, paternalism evokes a positive feeling signifying a reciprocal relationship between a wealthy person of influence and a loyal client. Both need each other. However, this positive association between a benevolent authoritarian leader and a loyal follower might be changing.

The GLOBE study not only measured what managers thought was the *practice* of power distance in their organization, but also asked what they thought power distance *should* be. They compared the *practice* with the *value* of power distance. In every country surveyed they found that power distance was higher than people thought it should be. The countries with the highest power distance had the greatest desire for less power distance. Even in countries with a relatively low power distance, managers desired it to be even lower. "Managers in all cultures reported that their societies practice power distance more strongly than they believe they should."[22] One wonders if there is a growing universal desire for a more egalitarian society.

A recent *Wall Street Journal* article titled "Pulling Rank Gets Harder at One Korean Company" describes how a top-level manager in the SK Telecom Company used to be able to cut off discussion merely by declaring the debate over. Company managers then decided they needed a culture shift because profits were declining in their cell-phone market. They dissolved three levels of bureaucracy, changed the bonus system to reward productivity rather than seniority, and replaced the title of "manager" with "team leader." They felt that the high-power-distance system discouraged creativity and innovation. Under the new lower-power-distance culture, several new profitable products have been introduced by younger employees.[23]

Researchers in the GLOBE study reveal their bias when they report:

> One element of high power distance is clearly dysfunctional as it pre-empts the society from questioning, learning, and adapting as there is little opportunity for debate and voicing of divergent views. Asking questions may be interpreted or regarded as criticizing and blaming, and therefore may be prohibited. In contrast, within the low-power-distance cultures of the West, the flexible distribution of power is expected to facilitate entrepreneurial innovation, to allow broader participation in education, and to constrain the abuse of power and corruption.[24]

Both Hofstede and the GLOBE study report findings of strong positive correlations between high power distance and frequency of corruption.[25] Since most high-power-distance countries are not wealthy, it could be that poverty encourages corruption. Or it could be that countries with high power distance have fewer checks and balances, which then leads to corruption and poverty. The data from these studies is not adequate to support either hypothesis. Societies with high power distance also have less economic prosperity, life expectancy, social health, general satisfaction and gender equality.[26] Again, no one is sure which is the cause and which is the effect. It could be that the lack of economic prosperity and social health encourages people to desire a strong leader, or it could be that too much power in a leader leads to corruption and poverty. The fact that every country studied desired less power distance, and that countries with high power distance are beginning to change, suggests that high power distance is partly a symptom of a dysfunctional society.

I suspect that there is a correlation between power distance and context. Do people in high-context cultures prefer high-power-distance leaders, and do low-context cultures feel more at home with low-power-distance leaders? The hypothesis is worth testing.

## THE BIBLE AND POWER DISTANCE

Examples of both high- and low-power-distance cultures are found in the Bible. From a biblical perspective high power distance can be either good or bad.

Scripture describes the ultimate power distance between the Almighty God and human beings. Isaiah challenges the people with the question, "With whom, then, will you compare God?" (Is 40:18). He reminds Israel that God measures the waters with the hollow of his hand, his breath marks the heavens, he weighs the mountains and hills on scales, and the nations are like a drop in a bucket, or dust on the scales. The islands weigh as much as fine dust, people are like grasshoppers. This is the God who knows all the stars in all the galaxies by name (Is 40:12, 15, 22, 26). Such power distance is unimaginable to frail human beings. Yet this same God who calls the stars by name is our Father. He loves his children, and actually lives in us (Jn 14:23; 15:4). The God of the universe calls us friends (Jn 15:15)! The most transcendent being imaginable is more imminent than our closest friend. What an example of high and low power distance within the same person.

Miriam and Aaron questioned the authority of Moses by raising the low-power-distance question "Has the Lord spoken only through Moses?" (Num 12:2). Both Miriam and Aaron objected to the higher status of Moses and felt they should share his special relationship with the Lord. God's anger burned against Miriam and she became leprous. Later the sons of Korah rebelled against the leadership of Moses. They criticized Moses and Aaron for their high power distance, using the low-power-distance argument, "You have gone too far! The whole community is holy, every one of them, and the Lord is with them. Why then do you set yourselves above the Lord's assembly?" (Num 16:3). Again, the anger of the Lord burned against the followers of Korah for wanting to grab power from Moses. The earth split apart and swallowed the followers of Korah.

Several passages in the New Testament support high-power-distance values. Jesus taught that it was right to pay taxes to the hated hierarchical Roman government (Mk 12:17) and to pay the temple tax (Mt

17:27). Peter reminds younger believers to submit to their elders (1 Pet 5:5). Paul informs his friends in Rome to be subject to governing authorities (Rom 13:1). The writer of Hebrews challenges the congregation to "have confidence in your leaders and submit to their authority, because they keep watch over you as those who must give an account. Do this so that their work will be a joy, not a burden, for that would be of no benefit to you" (Heb 13:17).

At the same time, a biblical case can be made for low power distance. Jesus chides the high-power-distance Pharisees who relish the place of honor at banquets, seek the most important seats in the synagogue, love to be greeted with respect in the marketplace and insist that others honor them by their title, Rabbi (Mt 23:5-7). Jesus responds:

> But you are not to be called "Rabbi," for you have only one Master and you are all brothers. And do not call anyone on earth "father," for you have one Father, and he is in heaven. Nor are you to be called "teacher," for you have one Teacher, the Messiah. The greatest among you will be your servant. (Mt 23:8-11)

Jesus also criticized his disciples when they argued over who would capture the high-power-distance places of honor beside him. He challenged the high-power-distance values so pervasive in the culture.

> Jesus called them together and said, "You know that the rulers of the Gentiles lord it over them, and their high officials exercise authority over them. Not so with you. Instead, whoever wants to become great among you must be your servant, and whoever wants to be first must be your slave—just as the Son of Man did not come to be served, but to serve, and to give his life as a ransom for many." (Mt 20:25-28)

Paul reminded Timothy not to let anyone look down on him because he was young (1 Tim 4:12). In high-power-distance cultures, Timothy would have less status because of his youth. Paul challenged the high-power-distance culture in its lack of respect for youth.

In stark contrast to the culture of the day, and different than other, false teachers, Paul came to the church in Corinth with low-power distance, which he describes as "weakness with great fear and trembling" (1 Cor 2:3). False teachers came to Corinth with eloquent oratory skills and high-power-distance values, causing power-struggle divisions in the church. Paul intentionally promoted countercultural values by taking a low-power-distance position of weakness.

The Bible teaches respect for those in authority but also that those in authority must not demand to be held in high esteem. Leaders in high-power-distance cultures need to be aware of the dangers of pride in position and of lording it over followers. Followers in low-power-distance cultures need to show proper respect for those in authority over them. Both leaders and followers are to clothe themselves with humility toward one another, because "God opposes the proud but shows favor to the humble and oppressed" (1 Pet 5:5).

The Bible does not seem to give a clear answer to the question, "Which is better, high- or low-power-distance values?" The most obvious examples of power distance, hierarchy and status symbols come from the Old Testament, before the Holy Spirit was poured out on all believers, and before teachings on the priesthood of all believers.

The priesthood of all believers is a most astounding doctrinal development in the New Testament. No longer does the priesthood arise solely from the clan of Aaron in the tribe of Levi, but now people from every tribe in Israel and every nation on earth are called to a royal priesthood. Peter writes to God's elect, scattered exiles and calls them to be a holy priesthood, a chosen people and a royal priesthood (1 Pet 2:5, 9). John describes the new song sung by believers from every tribe, language, people and nation, calling these multicultural believers a kingdom of priests to serve God (Rev 5:9-10). The progress of revelation between the Old and New Testaments indicates a shift from higher to lower power-distance values.

Respect for authority, a high-power-distance value, is found in the Old Testament as well as in the Gospels and in the writings by Paul and Peter. But the Bible is filled with bad examples of high-power-distance leaders who arrogantly misuse power. Scripture teaches that followers should respect leaders and that leaders must not seek their own good, but the good of followers. This is not easy to do in a sinful world. The universality of the Fall predisposes leaders in every time and place to be tempted by pride and domination. The Bible stands in judgment of arrogant leadership in every culture. Scripture seems to leave room for some flexibility regarding power distance in leadership style but not in leadership attitudes. The heart of every leader must be humble, seeking the good of others and suspicious of one's own motives.

## IMPLICATIONS FOR LEADERSHIP IN THE GLOBAL CHURCH

Appreciating cultural differences regarding power distance will go a long way in promoting healthy interactions within the global body of Christ. Let's look at some of the practical implications.

*1. Church-to-church partnerships.* In the recent past, inexpensive air travel and Internet communication have led to the growing phenomenon of church-to-church partnerships. Most often the partnership is made up of churches in a wealthy nation partnering with a church in the developing world. An interesting dilemma emerges when churches realize that the term *partnership* has different connotations, depending on an understanding of power distance. Partnership in low-power-distance cultures assumes equality, but in high-power-distance cultures there must be a junior and a senior partner. High-power-distance partnerships presume a patron and client relationship.

I remember a church leader in the majority world describing the way he understood the partnership between his church and a Western church. His metaphor was that of a horse and rider, with the national church being the rider and the foreign church, the horse. The rider guides the horse and the horse provides the power. The metaphor makes sense in a high-power-distance society, but is anathema for low-power-distance leaders. Many Western churches seek an egalitarian partnership, while most churches in high-power-distance societies assume that their Western partner will have more or less power than themselves. The recognition that they have different assumptions and that neither culture is being devious will do much to avoid misunderstanding in partnership relationships.

Unfortunate misunderstandings are common when churches in low-power-distance cultures seek partnership relationships with high-power-distance churches. I remember when leaders in a small war-torn country wanted to partner with churches in the United States to build and staff a hospital. When the local leaders were asked what they would contribute to the partnership, they said, "We will provide the sick people, you provide the hospital." Such a partnership makes perfect sense in a society that expects and appreciates high-power-distance values.

Despite a genuine desire to be egalitarian, churches in high-power-distance and wealthy countries are subtly tempted to see themselves as patrons in a partnership relationship with churches in less wealthy countries. Leaders in poorer churches may even desire and appreciate the junior partner role. Frank discussions about power distance need to take place at the beginning of the partnership relationship.

*2. Sharing resources.* One of the most divisive issues in missions today is that of wealthy churches supporting pastors and missionaries in more needy areas of the world. Some make the case that supporting nationals is the only wise use of money, while others argue that supporting nationals will stifle local giving and create unhealthy dependency on temporary outside funding.[27]

Understanding power distance helps shed new light on the discussion. In high-power-distance societies, both giving and receiving churches assume and appreciate dependent patron-client relationships. Churches in low-power-distance cultures assume that paternalistic relationships are degrading and dehumanizing. Dialogue about power distance issues could stimulate understanding, self-awareness and trust in this debate.

*3. Church and mission relationships.* When missionaries initiate a new ministry with an unreached people group, a dependency relationship takes shape between the new believers and missionaries. This is to be expected. But when the new believers come from a high-power-distance culture, they may expect the missionary to be in charge for a long time. Sadly, high-power-distance missionaries may agree to stay in control. Misunderstandings are likely to arise when new believers wish to take more responsibility or when missionaries turn over responsibility to the local church and assume a lower power-distance relationship.

I served in a situation where the time came for the mission agency to transfer hospitals, schools, bookstores, property and ministries to the national church. The national church assumed that roles would be reversed: previously the church was under the control of the mission, so now the mission would be under the control of the church. The mission desired an equal partnership but soon realized that this concept was difficult to understand in a high-power-distance culture. When the missionaries explained that they wanted to work as brothers, church leaders asked, "Who is the elder brother?" The mission considered pulling out completely or beginning a separate organization in the country. Tensions grew. After several years of dialogue, national church leaders agreed to allow the mission a level of autonomy and the missionaries agreed to work under the leadership of the national church in church-related ministries. Learning to cooperate in spite of puzzlement over the subtle cultural value of power distance takes special grace, but when it works, the body of Christ moves ahead with fresh vigor.

*4. Multicultural teams.* One of the most encouraging developments in the global church is the movement of missionaries from every country in the world going out to serve in crosscultural situations everywhere. Yet the more multicultural the team, the greater the probability for misunderstandings about leadership and the greater the need for patient, humble understanding about power distance in leadership.[28]

I remember a challenging situation involving a multicultural team with a very high-power-distance director and some new enthusiastic missionaries from low-power-distance countries. The director was likable and genuinely cared for the newer missionaries. He lovingly micromanaged them, telling them where to live, when to study, how to minister and what food to eat. I suspect he gave them excellent advice. But his attitude stirred up rebellion among the missionaries. We tried sending various leaders from the respective sending countries to mediate the bitterness between missionaries, but the situation only worsened. I should have realized the problem in that one leader came from a very high-power-distance country, and the other from one of the lowest. Sadly, great damage was done. The situation did not change until a new director was appointed who understood the power-distance tension and taught grace between the multicultural missionaries. Today missionaries in that country have great respect for each other, and fresh vision has been rekindled.

*5. Decision making.* In low-power-distance cultures, decisions might be made at any level of the organization, but in high-power-distance societies the most important decisions must be made by the top leadership. The subtleties of power distance can confound even the most experienced missionaries. The following is a true story with the names changed.

Tom and Ann had just returned to Africa after their home assignment. Before their home assignment they had received verbal permission from the church leaders in the central office to do literature work. Having received verbal permission, Tom and Sue assumed that all levels of the church had been adequately informed and had given their approval. Upon arrival, however, the local church leader asked for a "formal" letter from the central office authorizing their ministry. Since Tom and Ann didn't have a formal letter, the local leader called the central office. He was told that no "official" discussions had taken place and that Tom and Ann should not be allowed to carry on their ministry until the meeting took place. It took over three months before a meeting could be organized to formalize their ministry.

What was happening here? It seems that various customs clashed to cause this misunderstanding. Tom and Ann thought that face-to-face discussion was all that was needed to gain approval for their ministry. They had discussed the assignment with all levels of the church, so they assumed a formal permission had been given. Actually, there was "approval in principle" but not formal approval. They learned that only the top leader could give formal approval, not the department heads. Since the top leader had not granted approval, the previous discussions were not binding. It was also essential to call a formal meeting of all parties involved. So although each individual had given approval, all the leaders together had to approve the decision. After this, a formal letter was written, complete with an official stamp.

## RETHINKING THE PARADOX

One morning during my first weeks in Nigeria, I was peddling my new chrome Raleigh to work. At twenty-three years of age, I directed the Christian Education Department for a fast-growing denomination. I wanted to be a servant leader, and I felt that my three-speed bike allowed me to identify more closely with common people. However, on this morning, I was stopped by a highly respected pastor who proceeded to chide me for riding my bicycle. I brought shame to the denomination, he declared. Here I was, a high-ranking department head, and I didn't even own a car. My mind raced in protest. My wife and I were fresh out of graduate school with no savings. We had raised the basic support and headed off to Nigeria without the additional funds needed for a car. I smiled and told him that we were looking into buying a used Volkswagen Beetle. He immediately objected that a Volkswagen was not appropriate either. I needed at least a Peugeot 404, but even better a 504. I was stunned. First, we didn't have enough money for a Volkswagen, let alone a Peugeot. Second, even if we did have enough money I wanted to be a servant leader who identified with the majority of the people. Was I wrong—a slave to my own cultural myopia—or was the pastor misguided by unbiblical values of status?

Few things about leadership are more interesting, frustrating, challenging and rewarding than the study of cultural values. I distinctly remember my first exposure to the idea of cultural values in a biculturalism class from Marvin Mayers at Wheaton Graduate School. I felt that I had just discovered another set of eyes. Suddenly hundreds of the things that puzzled me as a missionary in Nigeria made sense. Traffic patterns, church services, committee meetings and financial statements took on new light as I reflected on basic values about time, goals, prestige, vulnerability and dichotomies.[29] I went back to Nigeria with fresh insights into perplexing situations. I realized again that "there is nothing as practical as good theory." I came to understand that the elderly pastor who was offended by my bicycle was expressing a culturally influenced view of prestige and status.

Power distance is a theological and practical paradox. We are often reminded in Scripture both to respect those in authority over us and to submit mutually to one another in the family and the church. "The elders who direct the affairs of the church well are worthy of double honor, especially those whose work is preaching and teaching" (1 Tim 5:17). This points to high-power-distance values. Yet the primary metaphor of the church is that of a body, where no one part can say to another "I don't need you," and no one can say, "I don't belong" (1 Cor 12:12-31). In Christ no one should have an inferiority complex, nor should anyone have a superiority complex. It seems that major problems arose among Jesus' disciples and later in the early church over the misuse of power. In Corinth, quarrels arose because some followed Apollos, others Cephas and still others boldly proclaimed that they followed Christ. High-power-distance leadership was a major problem for the church in Corinth.

The solution to the paradox leads to a new way of looking at leadership. All of us in the body of Christ, no matter what our formal position, must love and obey the Lord while we honor and submit to one another in love. If we follow this principle, we can adapt to different cultural values in the way we lead and the way we follow.

When a leadership value contradicts the clear universal teaching of Scripture, we need to lovingly confront that practice in a culturally relevant manner and graciously teach the Word in the power of the Spirit so that the Lord will convict.

In areas that do not contradict Scripture, the bicultural leader will follow the admonition of the apostle Paul: "I have become all things to all people so that by all possible means I might save some" (1 Cor 9:22).

To be aware of underlying cultural values does not resolve all the misunderstandings of leadership, but it helps. When the elderly pastor in Nigeria disapproved of me for riding a bicycle, I had doubts about his motivation and didn't understand why he was critical of me. I was proud of living a frugal lifestyle and of identifying with the local people even though I had come from a part of the world where most adults owned automobiles. By riding a bicycle I could greet all the people on the road and improve my Hausa language ability. I found myself wondering if the pastor was materialistic or if he perhaps wanted me to provide a taxi service for him. I realize now that he was actually trying to help me by making my ministry more credible in the eyes of the local people. Perhaps he was also trying to help me realize that by riding a bicycle instead of driving a Peugeot 504, I was degrading the image of the other Nigerian church leaders.

Where the Bible does not give clear principles, we must extend grace toward others. When the Bible is not clear about a leadership style, it is unbiblical to become dogmatic about that preference.

While I served as international director of SIM, I had two business cards printed, one for low-power-distance cultures and the other for high-power-distance cultures. Above the contact information, the low-power-distance card merely read "Jim Plueddemann." The high-power-distance card read, "James E. Plueddemann, Ph.D., International Director."

As I preached my sermon in the large Korean church, I thanked the Lord for the highly respected pastor who helped me gain credibility with the congregation by providing me with an ordained translator.

# REFLECTIONS ON
# MULTICULTURAL LEADERSHIP[30]

Oscar Muriu, Pastor, Nairobi Chapel, Kenya

Americans have two great things going for them culturally.One is that Americans are problem-solvers. Every time I come to the U.S., I like to spend a couple hours in a Wal-Mart. I find solutions to problems that I never thought of!

The rest of the world, even Europe, isn't so intent on solving inconveniences. We tend to live with our problems. Americans don't easily live with a problem—they want to solve the problem and move on.

The second great thing for Americans is that the educational system teaches people to think and to express themselves. So a child who talks and asserts himself in conversation is actually awarded higher marks than the one who sits quietly.

Those two things that are such great gifts in the home context become a curse when you go into missions. Americans come to Africa, and they want to solve Africa. But you can't solve Africa. It's much too complex for that. And that really frustrates Americans.

And the assertiveness Americans are taught in school becomes a curse on the field. I often say to American missionaries, "When the American speaks, the conversation is over." The American is usually the most powerful voice at the table. And when the most powerful voice gives its opinion, the conversation is over.

Americans find that almost impossible. They do not know how to hold their tongue. They sit there squirming, because they're conditioned to express their opinions. It's a strength at home, but it becomes a curse on the field.

In a sense Western missions has been marked by that. But isn't it strange that Jesus not only entered society incarnate at the weakest point, as a defenseless child who needed the care of his host community, but he also told his disciples: "Do not go with money; do not go with a second pair of shoes; go in a stance of vulnerability; be dependent on the communities you visit"? Isn't it interesting that for thirty years he doesn't speak out; doesn't reveal himself; he remains quiet, and only after thirty years of listening and learning the culture does he begin to speak.

# LEADERSHIP AND INDIVIDUALISM

*My brother and me against my cousin,*
*my cousin and me against the stranger.*

MIDDLE EASTERN PROVERB

THE MAJESTIC ANDES MOUNTAINS towered above us as we held a vision seminar with a group of highly gifted and motivated missionaries. This was a multicultural team composed of Germans, Latin Americans, North Americans and Australians. On the first morning I asked each of them to reflect prayerfully on their personal visions—their hopes and dreams for their ministry in the country. I asked, "If God were to richly bless your ministry, what might it look like in the next five to ten years?" I sent the team members into the mountains for the rest of the morning to pray and reflect on my question. In the afternoon we returned to share our personal visions with one another. The individual vision statements were outstanding, reflecting innovation and the personal giftedness of these talented people. As we sat in a circle and listened to each other, I tried to find clusters of common interest so we could build a teamwide vision statement. But the longer I listened, the harder it was to discover a common purpose. How could it be that such a talented group of culturally astute missionaries were not integrating with each other in ministry?

The lack of collaboration frustrated some of the missionaries, but others didn't see a problem with not having a common purpose. As I looked around the circle, it struck me that most of this multicultural team came from countries with highly individualistic cultural values. Yes, they were friends, but each personal ministry was completely separate from the others. Only two couples were discouraged by the lack of cooperation, and I noticed that they came from countries that placed a high value on collectivism.

The group members realized their problem, but weren't sure what to do about it. They decided to continue meeting and to think and pray about a common vision that would incorporate the unique giftedness of each individual. The results were dramatic. Over the next year they worked out a fresh vision and strategy that allowed their ministries to overlap without stifling the talents of individuals. The refocused vision led to radical changes in their activities. They decided to discontinue some ministries and begin other new initiatives that would better integrate the strengths of the team. They became a delightful example of how a group of individualistic missionaries from diverse cultures can unite in vision without losing the distinctiveness of each person.

## THE DILEMMA

Does the community exist to meet the needs of individuals, or should individuals seek to foster the good of the group?

Some cultures place a high value on the community and others on the individual. Parents in some societies raise their children to be independent by the age of twenty-one, while others raise their children to be lifelong and loyal family members. Sociologists label the difference as *individualism* and *collectivism*. While cultures are a mixture of both, they tend to place a stronger emphasis on one or the other.

Trompenaars and Hampden-Turner describe the dilemma between individualism and collectivism. "The individualist culture sees the individual as 'the end' and improvements to communal arrangements as the means to achieve it. The communitarian culture sees the group as its end and improvements to individual capacities as a means to that end."[1] They describe the dilemma as a cycle. Individualism promotes personal freedom and responsibility, but leads to self-centeredness. The cure for self-centeredness is the establishment of communitarian values and group consensus, which in turn leads to conformism and slow decision making which then takes one back to individualism.[2]

As I finished a presentation on teamwork in New Zealand, a young missionary candidate thanked me for the talk. He especially liked the concept of team. I asked if he would be willing to let an experienced team guide his ministry? Without hesitation he exclaimed, "Oh no! I don't want other people telling me how to do my ministry." When I asked what he would want a team to do, he replied, "Help me find a place to live, help with my government papers and find a good language school for me." For this young man, the purpose of the group was to assist his individual ministry. Such thinking makes perfect sense in an individualistic culture, but would seem strange to missionary colleagues from a collectivistic society. The quandary takes on special significance as missionaries from dozens of cultures are thrown together to minister in scores of additional cultures.

Few cultural values are more fascinating or frustrating for leaders in the global church than individualism and collectivism. Many pastors and missionaries from the majority world value the group over the individual, while many in the West assume the primacy of the individual over the group. One of my former students from Japan quoted a proverb taught to her by her parents: "The nail that sticks up is the one that is pounded." Duane Elmer quotes an African proverb in his book *Cross-Cultural Connections:* "If you want to travel fast, go alone. If you want to travel far, go together."[3] Such proverbs make perfect sense in collectivistic cultures, but sound quaint in individualistic cultures where being distinctive is of utmost value. The truth is that individuals need one another in order to become fully human, but an overly domineering community will stifle personal development.

## INDIVIDUALISM/COLLECTIVISM RESEARCH

Theorists have investigated the dilemma of individualism and collectivism as seen from the beginning of civilization. Several have suggested that in order to survive, scattered families of nomadic people taught the value of individual responsibility. But as groups came together to form villages, towns and cities, the need grew for cooperation and collective responsibility. In 1700 b.c., the Babylonian Code of Hammurabi protected the rights of society over the individual.[4] Through the Ten Commandments, God gave Moses regulations about how people should relate to God and to each other. The community was commanded to worship God alone and to honor parents. They were not permitted to murder, commit adultery, steal, give false testimony or covet. These laws set standards for community life and only secondarily for individual rights. Even today nomadic herders and fishermen tend to place a higher value on individual responsibility, while those living closer together on farms, in villages and towns require collective cooperation. The movement of people into impersonal mega-cities may lead to a resurgence of individualism.

Crosscultural studies on individualism and collectivism are prolific and fascinating. We will look at several major studies.

Trompenaars and Hampden-Turner define "individualism as a prime orientation to the self, and communitarianism as a prime orientation to common goals and objectives."[5] They administered a questionnaire to 30,000 managers in forty countries. One question asked:

> Which kind of job is found more frequently in your organization?
> A. Everybody works together and you do not get individual credit.
> B. Everybody is allowed to work individually and individual credit can be received.[6]

They found that in general, countries in Asia and the Middle East tended toward the collectivistic value of working together, while several of the eastern and northern European countries tended toward individualism. But the data is mixed, with Romania and Denmark scoring toward the collectivistic end of the scale. While they found large national differences, regional variations are hard to detect in this research.[7]

Hofstede reported that "the vast majority of people in our world live in societies in which the interest of the group prevails over the interest of the individual. We will call these societies collectivist."[8] In these societies the desires of the extended family are more important than those of the individual. The close-knit family usually includes parents, siblings, grandparents, aunts, uncles and cousins. "Therefore one owes lifelong loyalty to one's in-group, and breaking this loyalty is one of the worst things a person can do. Between the person and the in-group a mutual dependence relationship develops that is both practical and psychological."[9]

Hofstede continues, "A minority of people in our world live in societies in which the interests of the individual prevail over the interests of the group, societies that we will call individualist."[10] Children in individualist societies are usually born into a nuclear family made up of only parents and siblings. Children are taught to be independent, to do things for themselves and to have a personal identity. Grown children are expected to move away and live on their own, often in distant locations.

The findings of Hofstede place the United States, Australia, Great Britain and Canada high on individualism along with most European countries. Japan, India, Brazil and many Middle Eastern countries are near the middle of the scale. China, Africa and most Asian and Latin American countries are the least individualistic.[11]

The GLOBE study investigated a more complex understanding of collectivism and individualism. The study looked at in-group and institutional collectivism.[12] To measure in-group collectivism, respondents were asked how strongly they agreed or disagreed with the statement: "In this society, children take pride in the individual accomplishments of their parents." To measure institutional collectivism respondents were asked how strongly they agreed or disagreed with this statement: "In this society, leaders encourage group loyalty even if individual goals suffer." Researchers also asked respondents to differentiate between the current practice of collectivism and what they thought the value should be. They asked how leaders practice group loyalty and how they *should* encourage group loyalty.

In-group collectivism scores were highest in Southern Asia, the Middle East, Eastern Europe, Latin America and Confucian Asia.

Middle score values were found in Africa and Latin Europe, with low collectivism scores in Anglo,[13] Germanic and Nordic Europe.[14]

Interestingly, there is not a strong correlation between how people rank themselves in their current *practice* and what they think their culture *should* be. For example, the Anglo respondents rated their *practice* of in-group collectivism as low but *valued* high collectivism. It is fascinating that Americans see themselves as individualists, but report that they would like to be more collectivist. People from China, India and Japan perceive themselves as collectivistic in practice but put more value on individualism. There are likely to be major shifts in cultural values in coming generations.[15] Differences between the way people currently see themselves and what they think they should be challenge our stereotypes.

Deep-rooted cultural values are slow to change. In his book *Outliers,* Malcolm Gladwell observes the long-lasting effects of cultural legacies in the collectivistic "culture of honor."[16] He attributes the devastating family feuds in the Appalachian mountains in the United States to the Scotch-Irish herdsman heritage. "The survival of farmers depends on the cooperation of others in the community. But a herdsman is off by himself . . . under constant threat of ruin through the loss of his animals. . . . He has to be willing to fight in response to even the slightest challenge to his reputation."[17] He concludes, "Cultural legacies are powerful forces. They have deep roots and long lives. They persist generation after generation, virtually intact."[18] Blood feuds from Scotland and Ireland traveled with immigrants in the early 1800s in the Appalachian mountains and were still observed in research conducted at the University of Michigan into the 1990s.[19]

While we may not see family feuds in crosscultural teams, cultural legacies will likely influence the modern missionary movement for several generations.

One can easily imagine the puzzling situations arising as missionaries from highly individualistic societies team up with missionaries who have strong collectivistic values, such as missionaries from Switzerland and Ecuador ministering together in India. Their understanding of what it means to be a team may be radically different.

## POWER DISTANCE AND INDIVIDUALISM/COLLECTIVISM

"Large power-distance countries are also likely to be more collectivist, and small power-distance countries to be more individualist."[20] The countries highest on the individualism scale such as the United States, Australia, Great Britain, Canada and New Zealand also are lowest in power distance. Countries high in collectivism such as China, West Africa, Indonesia, Singapore, Venezuela and Ecuador are also the highest in power distance. The correlation is significant. There are exceptions though. Costa Rica ranked high in collectivism but fairly low in power distance, while French-speaking Europe tended toward larger power distance and high individualism.

Missionaries from individualistic, low-power-distance Australia and the United States would likely expect their team leader to be a "regular" member of the team, without special status or perks. On the other hand, missionaries from collectivistic, high-power-distance West Africa and South Korea might expect their team leader to have special charisma and higher educational qualifications. The leadership challenge comes when missionaries from, say, Senegal team up with missionaries from Australia. Both groups need to understand and appreciate each other's cultural values and pray for grace to compromise.

### SHAME AND GUILT

Because harmony is important in collectivistic cultures, *shame*, or the show of public displeasure, is a powerful motivator for proper behavior. On the other hand, "Individualist societies have been described as *guilt* cultures: persons who infringe upon the rules of society will often feel guilty, ridden by an individually developed conscience that functions as a private inner pilot."[21] Hofstede writes that shame is public and guilt is private. Shame results when members of the society know that a person has gone against the standards of the community, whereas guilt results when an individual does not live up to internal principles. The threat of losing face through public humiliation is a powerful motivator in a shame-oriented, collectivistic society. Gaining face, or public honor, is also important in a collectivistic society. Personal self-respect is the driving force in a guilt-oriented individualistic society.

Paul Hiebert describes the relationship between individualism and collectivism in shame and guilt cultures.[22] Hiebert defines guilt as "a feeling that arises when we violate the absolute standards of morality within us, when we violate our conscience. A person may suffer from guilt even though no one else knows of her or his misdeed."[23] Shame, on the other hand "is a reaction to other people's criticism, an acute personal chagrin at our failure to live up to our obligations and the expectations others have of us. . . . Self-respect is maintained not by choosing what is good rather than what is evil, but by choosing what is expected of one."[24] Hiebert maintains that a biblical view of sin is tied to both shame and guilt.

Serious misunderstandings arise when leaders from individualistic-guilt-oriented cultures seek to motivate, encourage or evaluate people from collectivistic-shame-oriented cultures. A director from individualistic Britain may bring shame to a collectivistic Chinese team member even when attempting to praise her. The opposite also is the cause for confusion. A collectivistic Ghanaian pastor may be so concerned about not bringing shame to a short-term team from individualistic America that he may not give needed suggestions for improving that team's ministry.

## INDIVIDUALISM/COLLECTIVISM AND MANAGEMENT

Hofstede describes implications of this concept for management practice. "In a collectivistic culture an employer never hires just an individual, but rather a person who belongs to an in-group."[25] In these societies it is desirable to hire a family member, someone who is already a member of the company or someone from a highly respected family. "The relationship between employer and employee is seen in moral terms. It resembles a family relationship with mutual obligations of protection in exchange for loyalty. Poor performance of an employee is no reason for dismissal; one does not dismiss one's child."[26]

Nepotism, or the hiring of family members, is often illegal or considered inappropriate in individualistic societies. "Conflict of interest" is thought to be a danger when family members work together. The association is a contractual agreement rather than a family relationship, and thus employees can be hired or fired based on individual performance. The personal appraisal interview is an evaluation technique invented by individualistic societies. Evaluation in collectivistic societies measures the effectiveness of the group and not the individual. The concept of 360-degree evaluation, or evaluation of individuals by superiors, colleagues and subordinates, would seem outlandish in societies with collectivism and high-power-distance values. The same is true for leaders who attempt to foster the sharing of honest feelings about other employees. "Sensitivity training, encounter groups, or transactional analysis, are unfit for use in collectivist cultures."[27]

In an individualist culture, accomplishing a task is more important than building relationships, whereas in collectivist cultures fostering relationships is the means for accomplishing the task.

## STAGES OF INDIVIDUALISM AND COLLECTIVISM

A slight modification of the Middle Eastern proverb illustrates possible stages of development for individualism and collectivism. *"Me against my brother, my brother and me against my cousin, my cousin and me against the stranger."* The individualist is against his brother, but the two brothers form a narrow collectivism which leads to a broader collectivism that will include a cousin. The proverb could continue to proclaim: "my brothers and cousins against closely-related clans, and related clans against distant clans."

I suspect that the worldview of leaders develops in phases as horizons expand from *ego-centric* individualism to *world-centric* collectivism. Just as a pebble makes ever-widening ripples in a smooth pond, leaders grow as their perspectives expand.

The development of worldview in leaders does not seem to progress in distinct or abrupt stages as if one were moving away from an immature stage to a more advanced one. The most distant ripples in the pond integrate all the previous waves. The center stays the same while the circles continue to move outward. In the same way, leaders with the broadest perspectives can still understand and utilize the earliest stages.

Babies do not abruptly grow into adults, and the worldview development of leaders is also gradual.

Global-centric

Ethnocentric

Family-centric

Egocentric
Individualism

Collectivism

Collectivism

Collectivism/Individualism

**Figure 7.1**

*Stage 1: Egocentric individualism.* The size of the ripple-circle for a newborn baby is extremely small. The whole universe is tied up in the *egocentric*, existential here-and-now. Since babies are egocentric, we don't blame them for being narrowly individualistic. This is a perfectly normal stage of development. Immaturity is not a problem for babies, but will become a serious challenge if individuals remain stuck in egocentrism. Egocentric individualism is a good and necessary first developmental step. Without an individual sense of identity a person would not be able to make a contribution to a group.

A leader functioning from the immature perspective of egocentric individualism assumes that the organization exists for her or his benefit. While appropriate for an infant, it will always lead to strife when found in adult leaders. I expect that many leadership tensions in the home, workplace and in the global church result from such leaders. They may even claim to be servant leaders, but in fact they serve others for their own selfish ends. Jesus described bad shepherds as those who abandon the sheep when the wolf comes, because they care nothing for the sheep. It seems that many shepherds are not good leaders because they primarily care for themselves. As egocentric leaders climb the ladder of success, they often dislodge others on the way up.

Egocentric leaders can develop broadened horizons as they move from family to clan to larger society, but in this stage they never lose the orientation of being at the center of their universe. They are now able to manipulate a wider horizon of people for their own ends. Such growth is really pseudo-development, or growth in immaturity.

**Stage 2: Family-centric collectivism.** As children develop they begin to see the world through the eyes of parents, siblings, grandparents and others in the household. The ripples in the pond of their worldview expand outward to include both the nuclear and extended families. As children learn that they are not the center of the universe, their egocentrism develops into a broader *family-centric* perspective. The individualism of babyhood moves into a wider collectivism of family. This too is a normal and healthy stage of development. Families are one of God's blessings. Over time, children become less self-centered, looking out for the needs of parents, siblings, grandparents, aunts and uncles.

Family-centric leaders have a genuine concern for the extended family and are even willing to sacrifice their own lives for the sake of their relatives. The self becomes intertwined with others. Stage 2 leadership is caring, sacrificial and paternalistic within the family circle.

While family-centric leadership is an improvement over egocentric, the limitations become evident through the "us versus them" mentality. Pastors seek to grow their little church in competition with other churches. A youth pastor may have a passion for the youth in the church, but not have a vision for how the youth ministry fits into the broader vision of the whole church. In Christian organizations, "turf protection," or the desire to see one's own department or committee gain resources to the detriment of other departments, is all too common. Leaders seek advantages for their circle even if this means hurting the larger organization.

***Stage 3: Ethnocentric collectivism.*** The horizons of young teens grow ever wider to include peers outside their family—other families, neighbors, distant relatives and those in neighboring towns. *Family-centrism* expands into *ethnocentrism,* the viewpoint that all the people I know are the center of the universe. An ethnocentric viewpoint is broader than a family- or ego-centered universe. There are probably levels of ethnocentrism, moving from the narrow collectivism of my family, my village, to my clan, my state, my country or my race. There may be dozens of ever-expanding circles as the ripples in the pond expand outward.

The ethnocentric leader has a broader perspective than the family-centric leader. A pastor may see the church as one of many in the community and seek the good of the whole denomination. The church may form alliances with churches in the community and become interested in global partnerships. While the ethnocentric leader has weaknesses, the growth in perspective is a welcome development.

Still, the ethnocentric leader has limitations. As pastors and missionaries reach out to the rest of the world, they will do so from the perspective of the leadership values of their own culture and assume that what they have learned about successful churches will apply to all cultures. This attitude can cause tensions with global church-to-church partnerships. Because of their limited perspectives, crosscultural workers assume that their cultural values are biblical and universal. The ethnocentric pastor of a megachurch in one culture will assume that the principles of success in his or her church are effective in any culture.

The strength of collectivism is the sense of belonging and the desire to live for others. The danger of collectivism is that it inevitably creates an *us-them* mentality. People in one's own family or community are treated with respect and care, but all too often those outside the ethnic circle are perceived as inferior or even as the enemy deserving to be cheated and oppressed.

***Stage 4: Global-centric collectivism.*** It's not possible for us as mere humans to see the people of the whole world as God sees them, but we can try. As children we memorized John 3:16, "For God so loved the world . . . " God's horizons incorporate individuals, families and all nations in a *global-centric collectivism* that outgrows the "us versus them" mentality—the temptation to love our friends and disdain our enemies.

There are several ways to describe this stage. To see the world from God's perspective is *theo-centric collectivism.* Because theocentric collectivism is uncommon, a leader who begins to see the world from this perspective might seem to be an individualist going against the norms of society and the narrow perspective of ethnocentric collectivism. But such a leader would actually be a *principle-centered individualist,* not an egocentric individualist. The distinction between individualism and collectivism becomes fused at this global-centric stage. The individual becomes fully alive, and the community breaks out of the narrow boundaries of the us-them mentality.

After the resurrection, Jesus' disciples were commanded by the Pharisee leaders to stop preaching the risen Christ. The disciples challenged the laws of their collectivistic society by responding, "We must obey God rather than human beings" (Acts 5:29). God's principles demand a higher allegiance than the rules of society. By going against the precedents established by Jewish religious laws, the disciples might have seemed to be reverting to individualism, but in fact they had progressed to a global-centric perspective. Few of the Jewish leaders ever understood the idea that Gentiles could be "right with God" without first becoming Jews.

Often global-centric leaders have been misunderstood. Martin Luther King Jr. had a principle-based leadership perspective when he proclaimed his dream:

> I have a dream that my four little children will one day live in a nation where they will not be judged by the color of their skin but by the content of their character. . . . And when this happens, when we allow freedom to ring, when we let it ring from every village and every hamlet, from every state and every city, we will be able to speed up that day when *all* of God's children, black men and white men, Jews and Gentiles, Protestants and Catholics, will be able to join hands and sing in the words of the old Negro spiritual: *Free at last! Free at last! Thank God Almighty, we are free at last!*[28]

# REFLECTIONS ON MULTICULTURAL LEADERSHIP

Dr. Desta Langena, Director of Missionary Training School in Ethiopia

For many years I struggled with the stereotypes we have of leadership without recognizing that leadership is a gift of the Holy Spirit. We can be sure that the Holy Spirit gives this gift of leadership wherever and whenever it is needed, including in newly planted churches.

I am so thankful to SIM missionaries who came to Durame, Ethiopia—especially Ralph Jacobson and Gauss Kayser, who labored mightily in pouring all their energy and every possible effort to help the Kambatta and Hadiya church in the two major areas of leadership and evangelistic training. I call such training *missiological leadership training.*

Ralph Jacobson conducted Church Leadership training classes on every Tuesday for the leaders and every Friday for the future leaders (the youth). Gauss Kayser presented a forceful Great Commission teaching in the Bible School. The effort of these two godly people and others who made sacrificial efforts made the Kambatta and Hadiya church to be very strong to this day.

Currently the Kambatta and Hadiya church has sent out over three hundred crosscultural missionaries. The former and current general secretaries (Dr. Mulatu Baffa and Dr. Tesfaye Yacob) of the Ethiopian Kale Heywet Church denomination are from this church. I believe that it is not because the Kambatta and Hadiya Church is braver than other churches or that it has a unique leadership genius of some kind. It is because of the very solid leadership foundation and mission mindedness established by godly missionaries in the early days that it is still operating in amazing ways—regionally, nationally and globally. I am also the product of that church.

From the very beginning of church planting, missionaries and intercultural leaders need to prayerfully investigate and recruit gifted leaders of any background and then provide them necessary leadership training. This kind of approach will develop strong intercultural leadership for future church planting movements.

I have also seen how God uses the trials of life to broaden and deepen a leader's perspectives. During the Communist regime in Ethiopia, God allowed a traumatic situation to shape me. The physical and mental torture in prison, the extreme pressure from family and society, and the dilemma of daily life made me a confused, frustrated, and weeping lad. During that time God taught me the importance of prayer, the significance of holiness, the meaning of commitment, the greatness and the value of the Bible, the mystery of ministry, and the beauty of his presence. When I abandoned everything to follow him, he became everything to me. By the help of his grace it is my covenant to live for him and to glorify him throughout my life.

# LEADERSHIP AND AMBIGUITY

*Leadership is an improvisational art.*

TOM PETERS

I WAS SWEATING—AND NOT JUST BECAUSE of the tropical heat. I was a third-term missionary, yet I was thoroughly confused. What was *really* going on as I chaired the board meeting for this Bible college in Nigeria?

I was delighted that the national church was taking responsibility for the administration of local Bible schools and was happy to be the only non-Nigerian at the table. As chair, I attempted to follow *Robert's Rules of Order* with motions, amendments and votes as we waded through decisions on budget, faculty, graduation requirements and financial aid. My puzzlement began as we approved the minutes of the previous meeting. I didn't remember voting on most of the recorded decisions. I was absolutely sure that I never promised to pay for fifteen bicycles for students to travel on practical work assignments. Admittedly, I had agreed that the bicycles were a good idea and that the school needed them, but how did the recording secretary understand that I had promised funding? I was sure that we never made a proper motion on the issue of bicycles. How could he record a decision without an official vote? What seemed ambiguous to me, coming from a low-context culture, was perfectly clear to the Nigerian board members. Each of them could sense the direction of the discussion about the bicycles and, without a formal vote, knew the decision.

Eventually I discarded *Robert's Rules of Order* because the motions became unimaginably confusing with dozens of amendments and amendments to amendments. No one wanted to vote until they could fully discuss the big picture, and by the time we voted no one knew the original motion. So instead, I would ask the recording secretary to read what he had written at the end of the discussion on each agenda item. Everyone seemed happy with this procedure. My Nigerian colleagues were teaching me to live with ambiguity.

Many people still live in traditional societies where everybody knows everybody, where people live their whole lives without ever meeting a stranger, and where life is predictable and stable. Even subtle nonverbal body language is completely understood by family and neighbors. In these high-context communities, folks sense what others are thinking. Edward T. Hall observes that for most of our history,

> our forefathers knew the significance of every act of all the individuals around them. . . . Living today in a rapidly changing, ever-shrinking world, it is hard for most of us to conceive what it would be like to grow up and live in a world that did not change, and where there were few strangers because one always saw and dealt with the same people. . . . People knew what was coming next before you did something or even that you were going to do it. "Jake is going to get a new horse." "Yup. He always fattens up the old one before he trades. Too cheap to feed 'em the rest of the time."[1]

Nevertheless, life is unpredictable in every culture. For some societies, ambiguity is a serious problem and leaders do everything they can to minimize it. They avoid uncertainty by attempting to predict and control the future. They set precise goals, make long-range plans, schedule appointments, design contingency plans, purchase insurance, make to-do lists and develop thick policy manuals. But not every society fears uncertainty. Leaders learn to live with ambiguity and with a laid-back attitude toward life. Communities with little desire to avoid uncertainty are puzzled by the stressful ways of those who do. On the other hand, leaders with a low tolerance for ambiguity can't understand the "whatever will be, will be" attitude toward life.

Cultural differences in avoiding uncertainty cause innumerable frustrations and puzzlements in leadership. As missionaries travel from everywhere to everywhere, local churches in every country are interacting with the rest of the world. Differences in the tolerance of ambiguity can lead to major misunderstandings. It seems that low-context cultures fear ambiguity, while high-context cultures take it for granted.

Imagine a pastor from Germany who wants to set up a short-term missions trip with a church in Latin America. The German pastor will want to know the precise goals of the trip, the exact time for the beginning and end of the journey, and an accurate prediction of how much the trip will cost. The Latin pastor may wait until the German team arrives to assign responsibilities. His decision will be based on getting to know the interests and abilities of the visitor. The German will probably be irritated by an apparent lack of planning, and the Latin will be perplexed by the German's obsession for controlling the future. Both are likely to be frustrated.

## RESEARCH ON UNCERTAINTY AVOIDANCE

Uncertainty is part of life. People living in societies with a low tolerance for ambiguity (high uncertainty avoidance) desire to minimize insecurity by having policies, time tables and detailed planning. Those living in societies with a high tolerance for ambiguity (low uncertainty avoidance) tend to live more in the present. Hofstede defines uncertainty avoidance as "the extent to which the members of a culture feel threatened by ambiguous or unknown situations. This feeling is, among other things, expressed through nervous stress and in a need for predictability: a need for written and unwritten rules."[2] His research found that societies with a strong desire to avoid uncertainty also experience higher levels of anxiety, resulting in higher rates of suicide and alcoholism. The study also revealed that older people are more likely to seek certainty. Cultures that value certainty appreciate rules, are more likely to obey laws, and people are more likely to stay in their jobs.[3]

Hofstede's general summary showed that people with a high tolerance for ambiguity accept uncertainty as a normal feature of life, experience less stress, show less aggression and have a relaxed family life,
with less respect for laws.[4]

The GLOBE (Global Leadership and Organizational Behavior Effectiveness) study investigated uncertainty avoidance in 62 societies,[5]
and defined uncertainty avoidance as "the extent to which members of
collectives seek orderliness, consistency, structure, formalized procedures, and laws to cover situations in their daily lives."[6] Their research
investigated the relationship between uncertainty avoidance and stress,
anxiety, the need for feedback, planning, innovation, accounting practices and perception of risk. All these have fascinating implications for
global cooperation in world missions.

Societies that avoid uncertainty tend to do the following:

- Formalize their interactions with others

- Document agreements in legal contracts

- Keep orderly and meticulous records

- Rely on formalized policies and procedures

- Establish and follow rules

- Verify communications in writing

- Take more moderate calculated risks

- Show stronger resistance to change

- Show less tolerance for breaking rules[7]

Societies that tolerate uncertainty tend to do these things:

- Be more informal in their interactions with others

- Rely on the word of those they trust rather than contractual
  arrangements

- Be less concerned with orderliness and maintenance of records

- Rely on informal interactions and informal norms rather than
  formalized policies, procedures and rules

- Be less calculating when taking risks

- Show less resistance to change
- Show less desire to establish rules to dictate behavior
- Show more tolerance for breaking rules[8]

The GLOBE study differed from the Hofstede research in that the former asked about uncertainty *practices* as well as *values*. For example, this question asked about *practice:* "In this society, societal requirements and instructions are spelled out in detail so citizens know what they are expected to do." Then they asked the similar *value* question: "I believe that societal requirements and instructions *should be* spelled out in detail so citizens know what they are expected to do."[9]

Interestingly, the researchers found a significant negative correlation between the way people describe their society and what they think it should be. People in high-certainty countries who live with tight societal requirements really wanted more flexibility, and those that tolerate uncertainty desired more structure. For example, Nigeria scored in the middle range in the *practice* of avoiding uncertainty, but had one of the highest scores with the *value* for avoiding uncertainty. Many Nigerians seem to be desiring more structure and predictability. At the other extreme, Switzerland was very high in the *practice* of avoiding uncertainty, but was last in *valuing* uncertainty. The Swiss have a lot of structure and predictability, but apparently many people want less regimentation.[10]

Regionally, Nordic and Germanic Europe scored the highest in avoiding uncertainty. The Middle East, Latin America and Eastern Europe had the lowest scores. Anglo, Asia, Africa and Latin Europe were in the middle.[11]

Avoiding uncertainty was also negatively correlated with power distance.[12] This makes sense. In low-power-distance societies it is more likely that the "law is king," whereas in high-power-distance societies "the king is law." The rule of law tends toward less uncertainty than the rule of a king.

Countries that avoid uncertainty tend to be more technologically developed,[13] have greater economic prosperity and support competition.[14] Does technology require people to have more structure? Are societies that fear the future more likely to seek technological solutions? Perhaps societies with more wealth can afford to take more steps to avoid uncertainty. This study showed that many people in high-tech countries wish for less structure, and those in low-tech countries wish for more. This insight has fascinating implications for multinational leadership strategies. Missionaries in multicultural teams may not actually desire the kind of leadership that is most prevalent in their home country.

Societies with a low tolerance for uncertainty (those with more rules) scored higher in admiration for democracy and desired more individual involvement in the political system.[15]

As expected, GLOBE researchers found a strong positive correlation between high uncertainty avoidance and future orientation. Societies seeking to avoid uncertainty tend to make detailed and long-range plans, whereas those more tolerant of ambiguity wait to see what might happen next. Perhaps those who live in cultures where they have little control of the future adapt to the unexpected.

As we look at research findings we typically ask:

1. Where do I fit on the scale? What does the data show about my country? From my experience, do the findings make sense?

2. Don't my values make more sense?

3. Isn't my way more biblical?

4. What are the implications of the data for multicultural teams, for church-to-church partnerships, and for leadership in international mission organizations? How will the research findings give practical input for world missions?

## THE BIBLICAL PARADOX

People living in societies that value certainty might be quick to point out the Bible verses supporting their position. After all, the Bible says that the wise will plan ahead and that we should count the cost and obey laws. On the other hand, people living in societies that tolerate ambiguity may point out the strengths of being "laid back" or "going with the flow" in a more relaxed, less stressful atmosphere. They too can quote verses about living by faith and not worrying about the future. Scripture can be found to support both certainty and uncertainty approaches to life. Balance is difficult. Are we supposed to avoid uncertainty through planning and goal setting on Monday, Wednesday and Friday, while rejoicing in ambiguity and living in the present on Tuesday, Thursday and Saturday? Does the Bible teach that we should be "control freaks" in some areas of our lives and "go with the flow" in others?

Let's look first at Scripture that supports the value of living with uncertainty.

- People with little tolerance for ambiguity attempt to control the future. God reminds us that he is in full control of the future. We aren't. In Isaiah, God says, "I make known the end from the beginning, from ancient times, what is still to come. I say, 'My purpose will stand, and I will do all that I please'" (Is 46:10).

- Anxiety is a prominent characteristic in societies with little tolerance for ambiguity. Jesus commanded, "Therefore do not worry about tomorrow, for tomorrow will worry about itself" (Mt 6:34). The passage tells us not to worry about what we will eat, drink, wear. We cannot add even one hour to our lives.

- When God told Abraham to leave his home, he "obeyed and went, even though he did not know where he was going" (Heb 11:8). Abraham had no precise goal or specified time frame, but he trusted God.

- "Trust in the LORD with all your heart and lean not on your own understanding; in all your ways submit to him, and he will make your paths straight" (Prov 3:5-6).

- People tend to insulate themselves from uncertainty by having a lot of money. But Paul teaches Timothy that those who are rich in this present world must not put their hope in wealth, which is uncertain, but to put their hope in God (1 Tim 6:17).

- The book of Proverbs is filled with reminders that while human beings think they control the future, God is in control of outcomes. "Many are the plans in a human heart, but it is the LORD's purpose that prevails" (Prov 19:21).

- People who hate ambiguity love the saying, "If you aim at nothing, you'll hit it every time," suggesting that smart people set precise objectives. There are no examples or admonitions in the Bible for leaders to set numerical goals within a specific time frame. This saying is not in the Bible.

Scriptures supporting the value of avoiding uncertainty:

- God knew that when human beings worked together, planned and set goals they could accomplish almost anything. That is why at the Tower of Babel God said, "If as one people speaking the same language they have begun to do this, then *nothing they plan to do will be impossible for them*" (Gen 11:6, italics added). Because God knew that people had such great potential for planning evil, he confused their language.

- Planning is a powerful way to avoid uncertainty. The book of Proverbs is filled with the admonition to plan. "Plans are established by seeking advice; so if you wage war, obtain guidance" (Prov 20:18). And again, "The plans of the diligent lead to profit as surely as haste leads to poverty" (Prov 21:5).

- Jesus commanded his followers to count the cost of discipleship. He gave the example of a wise builder estimating the cost of constructing a tower, and a wise king considering the possibility of going to war with an army twice as large as his (Lk 14:25-33). Only the foolish builder or general delights in ambiguity.

- Jesus understood the long-term plan for his life. The Gospel of John records many times when Jesus reminded his disciples that his time had not yet come. (Jesus talked about "his hour," or the time of his death in John 2:4; 7:6, 8, 30; 8:20; 13:1; 17:1.) Jesus was aware of the sequence of events in his life and planned his actions accordingly. He lived with the end in mind and was not ambiguous about his life's purpose.

- The apostle Paul was forced to live with ambiguity, but as much as possible he planned for the future. Apparently the church in Corinth accused Paul of not planning carefully. So he responded, "Was I fickle when I intended to do this? Or do I make my plans in a worldly manner so that in the same breath I say both 'Yes, yes' and 'No, no'?" (2 Cor 1:17). Paul went on to write that God is faithful and in him all the promises are "yes."

- The sluggard only lives for the present. The book of Proverbs is filled with criticisms of those who are too lazy to plan. The sluggard is told to go to the ant and learn how to store provisions at the harvest, even when there is no commander (Prov 6:6-8). Instead of planning for the future, the sluggard's life verse is, "A little sleep, a little slumber, a little folding of the hands to rest" (Prov 6:10), ignoring the fact that the next step is poverty. "Lazy hands make for poverty, but diligent hands bring wealth" (Prov 10:4).

### LIVING WITH BIBLICAL PARADOX

Most of us aren't comfortable with paradox, because paradox threatens both positions. Yet Scripture supports the argument for both trusting and planning, for resting and striving, for strategizing while trusting that God is in control of the outcomes.

- Faith is the bridge between the paradox of certainty and uncertainty. "Faith is being sure of what we hope for and certain of what we do not see" (Heb 11:1). From a human perspective, it seems absurd to be certain of what we cannot see. Yet this is what pleases God.

- Proverbs reminds us both to plan and to trust. "Commit to the LORD whatever you do, and he will establish your plans" (Prov 16:3). Leaders need plans, but only God can bring about results from those plans.

- Abraham lived by faith and often had to obey before he knew the purpose. God showed himself to him, giving him insights into a certain future. Abraham knew "for certain" that for four hundred years his descendants would be strangers in Egypt where they would be mistreated, but at the proper time they would come back to the land promised by the Lord (Gen 15:13-16). By faith, Abraham had no ambiguity about the future of his offspring.

- I'm impressed with the way Nehemiah lived with the paradox of ambiguity and planning. When the enemy threatened to attack while the walls were only half finished, Nehemiah both prayed and set a special guard (Neh 4:9). Leaders desiring to control the future on their own might set a watch, while other leaders might simply have a prayer meeting and go to sleep. Nehemiah did both: he prayed and he took action.

- Jesus told several parables that blend certainty and uncertainty. One of the most intriguing is a parable about the farmer who scattered seed and waited. "Night and day, whether he sleeps or gets up, the seed sprouts and grows, though he does not know how. All by itself the soil produces grain. . . . As soon as the grain is ripe, he puts the sickle to it, because the harvest has come" (Mk 4:27-29). The farmer had to plan ahead to prepare the soil, know when and how to scatter the seed, and be wise and hard-working at the time of the harvest. Even though the farmer did all he could to avoid uncertainty, he fully realized the mystery of the growing seed. In the same way, leaders in the kingdom of God must be responsible for taking initiative and planning as much as possible, but at the same time they trust the Lord of the harvest for the process and product of the harvest.

- We sometimes make a false dichotomy between working hard and trusting God. We assume that leaders who fear an uncertain future become workaholics, while those who trust God for the future become lazy. In the book of James, faith and works are two sides of the same coin. Abraham believed God and obeyed (Jas 2:21-24). The Bible is clear: leaders who have great faith are great women and men of action. There is no tension.

Paradox helps us to see dilemmas as fruitful tension. The constant interaction and blending of the two extremes brings about a healthy perspective. Leaders with too much fear of uncertainty can become legalistic and filled with stress. On the other hand, those with too little fear of uncertainty can become irresponsible and lazy. Scripture points to the healthy balance: trust and obey.

**IMPLICATIONS FOR LEADERSHIP IN THE GLOBAL CHURCH**

*Matching missionaries with ministries.* I've noticed that individuals with a farming background tend to be outstanding missionaries especially when ministering in rural ministry areas. My hunch is that farmers understand community and can live with uncertainty. They realize that they cannot control rainfall, the first frost or when baby lambs will be born. They work hard and are highly motivated, but they have learned to "go with the flow." Maybe this is why I've known so many effective missionaries from the farmlands of New Zealand, Canada and the United States. They've learned to work together and stay in close contact with the ever-unfolding situation around them and to be innovative when the unexpected happens.

I've also noticed that missionaries with business backgrounds in London or São Paulo have much in common with business people in Delhi. It seems that urban business people are more like urbanites halfway around the world than they are with rural people in their own country. To be successful they must plan, organize strategies and keep careful financial records. Their achievement requires a low tolerance for ambiguity.

I wonder if cultural differences regarding ambiguity are more related to differences in age, urban/rural living, or education and profession than they are to nationality. It makes sense to match peoples' values of uncertainty with appropriate ministries.

*Organization.* The Sudan Interior Mission began as missionaries from the United Kingdom, the United States and Canada were sent to Nigeria. The headquarters in Toronto probably ranked high on uncertainty avoidance, as leaders attempted to control the field from Canada. The general director told missionaries in Nigeria where to work and what to do from his desk in Toronto. Eventually the slowness of communication and the inappropriateness of some of the decisions led to a major shift in organizational structure. In 1915 the mission mandated that "decisions should be made as close to where they would be carried out as possible." The new flexibility led to better decisions, but decentralization gave mission leadership less control over uncertainty.

Hudson Taylor faced a similar scenario as his mission in London attempted to control decisions in China. The conflict led Taylor to form a new mission, the China Inland Mission, where field decisions were made in China.[16]

Few things reflect the cultural value of avoiding uncertainty as much as organizational structure. If an organization has no fear of uncertainty there is little need for structure, while organizations with little tolerance for ambiguity are highly organized. The challenge arises when mission societies or denominations seek to become truly multinational, resulting in partnerships between organizations that exhibit both high and low uncertainty-avoidance cultures. Suddenly the "one size fits all" mentality doesn't work. As world missions move "from everywhere to everywhere," organizational culture is likely to become more decentralized and ambiguous.

When I began my role as international director of SIM, we had a thick manual with policies for regulating almost everything. I remember spending hours in council meetings debating policies for "baggage allowance." How much "outfit" should be allowed for someone traveling 10,000 miles for four years, compared with a person going only 1,000 miles for two years? Should family size and age of children factor into baggage allowance? Such policies made a bit of sense when 90 percent of the missionaries traveled from the United States and Canada to West Africa, but later became too complicated in a multinational organization. In order to avoid future uncertainty, an isolated situation had led to a worldwide mandate. Thick manuals are helpful tools for avoiding uncertainty. But as a mission becomes multicultural, uniform policies are not appropriate for missionaries sent from Peru to China, Ethiopia to India, India to Sudan, or Senegal to Britain. The more SIM became truly multinational, the more monocultural guidelines became less useful. We needed a major cultural shift from an organizational structure with a centralized ethos to one that is more decentralized and comfortable with ambiguity.

I remember working for several years to establish a formal Sending Council in Korea. As the Korean board began to come together, the membership criteria of this group didn't fit the SIM policy manual, which stated that sending councils must be made up of business people, educators, women and lawyers as well as pastors. The Korean Council was totally composed of ordained male pastors. We soon realized that our model did not fit the Korean culture, and for the time being we needed to allow for flexibility.

I'm convinced that as mission organizations become more multicultural, they must aim for greater decentralization, allow for more local freedom and learn to live with ambiguity. If they attempt to avoid uncertainty through tight control, they will stifle cherished cultural values and remain monocultural. Many organizations will be hybrid organizations, with a wide range of decentralization.

The Lord has used mission organizations with all levels of centralization. The International Mission Board of the Southern Baptist Convention (IMB) of the United States is centralized and is able to make ministry changes quickly. Thus they were able to make a major shift from an emphasis on institutions (hospitals and Bible schools) to a sharp focus on evangelizing unreached people groups. Their new vision statement is "We will lead Southern Baptists to be on mission with God to bring all the peoples of the world to saving faith in Jesus Christ."[17] This across-the-board change in mission strategy would be difficult to implement in a decentralized mission.

At the other end of the continuum is Youth With A Mission. One of their values is "decentralization with accountability." From their website we read:

> Value 7. Be Broad-Structured and Decentralized
>
> YWAM is broad-structured and diverse, yet integrated. We are a global family of ministries held together by shared purpose, vision, values and relationship. We believe that structures should serve the people and the purposes of God. Every ministry at every level has the privilege and responsibility of accountability to a circle of elders, with overall international accountability to the YWAM Global Leadership Team.[18]

Though YWAM seems to be moving toward a more centralized organization, the current website describes their philosophy:

> As YWAM has grown over the years, YWAM's leaders have consistently sensed God leading them to develop as a family of ministries,

rather than a structured, centralized agency. Although we have main offices, we do not have an international administrative headquarters. Therefore each YWAM location is responsible for planning outreaches, initiating training programs, recruiting staff, financial resource development, and setting priorities in carrying out ministry.[19]

I recently had breakfast with a well-informed mission statesman and asked him about YWAM statistics. He smiled and said, "No one knows for sure how many missionaries they have, or if they have a consolidated worldwide budget." This approach is intentional and is one reason for YWAM's amazing multicultural growth.

I recently read a stimulating book called *The Starfish and the Spider: The Unstoppable Power of Leaderless Organizations*.[20] A "spider organization" avoids ambiguity by having a single leader at the top of the organization, an international headquarters and centralized structure. If you strike a spider on the head, it dies. Contrast the spider with the starfish. The "starfish organization" is fundamentally different.

> The starfish doesn't have a head. Its central body isn't even in charge. In fact, the major organs are replicated throughout each and every arm. If you cut the starfish in half, you'll be in for a surprise; the animal won't die, and pretty soon you'll have two starfish to deal with. . . . And with some varieties, the animal can replicate itself from just a single piece of an arm.[21]

The authors, Ori Brafman and Rod A. Beckstrom, begin their book by asking how the scattered and seeming unsophisticated Apache society could withstand the conquest of the Spanish forces. Hernando Cortés defeated the powerful Aztec nation by killing the head, Montezuma. But the Apache defeated the Spanish army because they were decentralized.[22] Their cultural traits were ambiguity, flexibility and shared power. Instead of a chief, the Apache had a Nant'an, or a spiritual leader, who led by example. Their leader Geronimo did not command an army and had no coercive power. He led through character and vision.[23]

The International Mission Board of the Southern Baptist Convention could be considered a spider organization, while Youth With A Mission could be described as a starfish organization. Spider organizations are funded by the organization, while starfish organizations are self-funded. IMB centrally funds missionaries, while missionaries with YWAM raise support. It is much easier to get statistics on the IMB than YWAM.[24] Both are great organizations. But YWAM is much more multicultural than IMB. YWAM has missionaries from over a hundred countries, while IMB is primarily a North American–run mission.

*The Age of Paradox*, a book by Charles Handy,[25] was extremely help-ful as we in SIM struggled with the ambiguity of decentralization for the sake of internationalization. If we decentralized too much, we were in danger of losing our vision and core values. If we decentralized too little, we would continue to be a Western-oriented mission agency and miss out on the way God is raising up missionaries from every country of the world.

We explored the concept of *federalism:*

> Federalism seeks to be both big in some things and small in others, to be centralized in some respects and decentralized in others. . . . It endeavors to maximize independence, provided that there is a neces-sary interdependence; to encourage difference, but within limits; it needs to maintain a strong center, but one devoted to the service of the parts; it can, and should, be led from the center but has to be managed by the parts.[26]

Related to federalism is Handy's description of *subsidiarity,* or the idea of "leaving power as close to the action as possible."[27] "The center's role is to orchestrate the broad strategic vision, develop the shared ad-ministrative and organizational infrastructure, and create the cultural glue which can create synergies."[28]

We looked at SIM as "a federation of villages." The headquarters helped to consolidate core values and focus the vision. Our attitude was to do whatever needed to be done to help our teams to be effective. We shortened the international manual and challenged each country to de-velop policies that would fit their cultural needs. We decentralized funding and strategic initiatives. Local leaders were challenged to take creative initiative to develop fresh ministries. I admit there were times when, as international director, I felt a country was moving outside of our core vision and I asked them to rethink their strategies and come back within the broad guidelines of the federation. The "federation of villages" concept may be a way for mission agencies to maintain some certainty while living with the unpredictable and delightful creativity of ambiguity.

The Lord has used both centralized and decentralized organizations in powerful ways. However, avoiding ambiguity through centralization will become much more difficult as mission agencies develop multicultural partnerships with sister organizations from around the world.

*Goals.* Missionary leaders from cultures that avoid uncertainty assume they must predict precise outcomes within a specified time frame. They dislike the ambiguity of vague goals. Not only do outcomes need to be exact, but the time frame also must be specified. For example, "Our goal is to plant ten churches in the next three years," or "We will distribute 15,000 pastors' book sets in China in the next 18 months."

As the year 2000 approached, many mission organizations set precise goals. Christian radio stations banded together to promote the goal of having at least one hour of broadcasting in every language group of over a million people by the year 2000. Note the precision of how many hours of broadcasting, to a certain-sized language group, by a certain date.

Mission organizations banded together for "The World by 2000" goal to plant a church in every people group. But such a goal was too fuzzy without added definitions. Missiologists wrote papers and held consultations to agree on a definition of "people group" and "church." Other organizations decided they wanted to evangelize every people group by the year 2000. But then they needed to define "evangelize."

Mission committees in high uncertainty-avoidance churches began to set comprehensive goals for their money. Many aimed to send 50 percent of their members on short-term trips or to partner with a church in the majority world in order to plant ten churches in five years.

Many good things result when churches and missions in low-tolerance-for-ambiguity cultures set precise goals. Goals motivate action and promote cooperation. I sensed a fresh enthusiasm and focus in local churches and mission agencies when they began to set goals. In SIM we contributed to the global radio strategy of "The World by 2000." The consultations challenged us to look for major gaps in global radio coverage and programming as well as unnecessary overlap and competition. While we didn't quite succeed in reaching our goal, the process helped us to be more effective and built lasting cooperative relationships.

While high uncertainty-avoidance goals are culturally appropriate for many missionaries, there are significant limitations.

As we bounced along a dusty road in a Land Rover, I could see that our missionary driver was discouraged. In fact he was ready to quit his ministry. The "Type A" highly motivated missionary from the United States was serving in a most challenging region of South America. Historically the area was called "the missionary graveyard." Missionaries spent lifetimes in ministry, seeing no results. After observing this ministry for a couple of days I asked him why he was so discouraged. He replied, "My goal was to plant a church with 100 baptized believers in my first term, or else stay home." I asked him how many new believers they had? "After three years, we have only 70 new believers, and I feel like a failure." I gasped. How could one of our most effective missionaries, fluent in Spanish with a blossoming church in a most resistant area, feel himself a failure? I gently tried to encourage him, reminding him of the amazing results the Lord had given so far. Thankfully he came back for several more terms, and the Lord blessed this area with more new churches and many new believers. Missionaries trying to avoid uncertainty may focus so narrowly on a precise goal that they miss the amazing things the Lord is doing in other areas.

Another limitation for uncertainty-avoiding goal-setters is that there is often a cultural mismatch between their values and those of the people they serve. For example, I once helped to facilitate a goal-setting course in Jos, Nigeria. Hausa-speaking pastors came on bicycles, busses and taxis to a seminar led by missiologists from the United Sates. The Americans began by handing out sheets of graph paper, asking the pastors to mark their church's attendance ten years ago, and then to put a dot on the graph for the church's attendance today. As they drew a line between the dots, they were asked to extend the line to find their goal for the next ten years. Some pastors suggested that their church membership should increase by fifty people a year. Then the seminar leaders asked pastors to chart this increase on logarithmic graph paper to show that the percentage of growth would actually decrease if they only added fifty members a year. Naturally the Hausa pastors were astounded that the curve began to bend downward even as their church continued to grow. At the end of the seminar they smiled and showed great appreciation for the outstanding lectures, but they didn't clearly understand them. Over the next ten years these same churches grew by about 300 percent and I'm sure the American experts took some of the credit.

This is not to say that churches with a high tolerance for ambiguity don't have goals. They do. But these goals are framed in terms of broad vision or a general direction. I worked with the Evangelical Missionary Society of the Evangelical Churches of West Africa (ECWA). I listened intently to the director, Rev. Panya Baba, as he challenged church members in a packed stadium to take the gospel to where it had not been preached before. With a powerful voice and dynamic hand motions, he pleaded, "We are debtors to Christ! We received the gospel free of charge, but now we are in debt and need to pay off our debt by taking the gospel to those who have never heard." The men responded with enthusiastic shouts and the women with a high-pitched "joy cry." Churches gave sacrificially and sent hundreds of crosscultural missionaries. These churches had a powerful vision of what God could do through them, but they didn't have projected numbers and dates. They were motivated by a God-given purpose.

*Planning.* It seems that mission agencies with a low tolerance for ambiguity do an excellent job of centralized planning. They think through details and anticipate problems before they happen. They set strict policies and have thick operation manuals. But too often they have "knowledge without zeal." On the other hand, agencies with a high tolerance for ambiguity may have great zeal, yet not be as concerned with planning.

SIM had traditionally been a mission agency that emphasized uncertainty avoidance. Our thick policy manual mandated minute details including rules "that toilets be kept as clean as possible" and "that monkeys shall not be kept as pets." As the mission has become more fully international, it has had to become more open to ambiguity. I met a pastor in Bolivia who longed for his church to be a missionary-sending church, so he began to investigate opportunities in Africa. He learned about a Spanish-speaking country, Equatorial Guinea. The pastor wanted to investigate ministry opportunities there, so he collected enough money to get him as far as Spain, where he had relatives. He didn't have enough funds to get from Spain to Equatorial Guinea, or to return to Bolivia, but he headed off to Spain anyway. With God's help he made it to Africa where he discovered that local churches wanted missionaries from South America. He eventually arrived back in Bolivia, recruited a missionary from the church, and divided the congregation into "12 Tribes." Each tribe was responsible for raising missionary support for one month. The last I heard, the church was ahead in its support requirement and the missionary was effective in Africa. Ministering with high tolerance for ambiguity seems strange to those who dislike uncertainty, but makes perfect sense to many of the emerging mission agencies from the church in the majority world.

## BUILDING GLOBAL UNDERSTANDING

It is interesting to note that the fastest growing churches in the world are usually in countries with high tolerance for uncertainty—those that don't set precise goals, plan long-range strategies or evaluate using precise numerical criteria. Church growth in Africa has been phenomenal. Churches in Ethiopia grew most rapidly during the Italian invasion and later during the Communist era.[29] Persecuted churches live in such ambiguous situations that they must tolerate uncertainty and fully trust God.

Missiologists from the Global South challenge the low-tolerance-for-ambiguity missiology of Europe and the United States. Missiologist Samuel Escobar criticizes what he describes as the "scientific" model of missions, a model that is tied to precise measurement.[30] In his presentation at the Iguassu Dialogue, Escobar described the future of evangelical missiology as moving away from what he terms "managerial missiology."[31] He made the claim that the future of missiology will go beyond the "post-imperial missiology"[32] that tries to reduce Christian mission to a "manageable enterprise."

Every characteristic of this missiology becomes understandable when perceived within the frame of that avowed quantifying intention. Concepts such as "people groups," "unreached peoples," "10/40 window," "adopt a people," and "territorial spirits" express both a sense of urgency and an effort to use every available instrument to make this possible.[33]

Mission agencies from cultures that seek to avoid uncertainty need to listen to the critique from Latin American missiologists. But in the same Iguassu Dialogue meetings, David Tai-Woong Lee from Korea graciously suggested less dichotomization between the models.[34] Each cultural value has advantages and disadvantages.

One of the difficulties of "managerial missiology" is that it tends to aim at the things that are easily predictable and measurable. Since it is less difficult to predict activities than outcomes, we are tempted to aim at what we can forecast, such as how many people heard the gospel and how many Bibles were distributed. Concerns for strengthening the spiritual qualities of a local church or fighting poverty are likely to frustrate those with a low tolerance for ambiguity.[35] Missions may not have been as consistently holistic as they should be because of the passion to avoid ambiguity. Holistic ministry is difficult to predict and quantify.

Emerging mission enterprises, where goals and detailed planning are often afterthoughts, are finding creative ways to send missionaries. Charlie Davis, the international director of TEAM mission, writes:

> A leader in Venezuela decided to challenge his church to send a bunch of people to take their vacation together in a town in Venezuela and share the gospel all week. That was the sum total of planning. Everyone arrived, found somewhere to hang their hammock, figured out how to eat after they arrived, and spent the afternoons and evenings hanging out with neighbors. They saw over 100 people come to Christ. It would have driven any of us uncertainty avoidance people up the wall.[36]

Both high- and low-uncertainty-avoidance mission enterprises have important strengths and significant weaknesses. We need each other. We need to listen to each other and blend an unchanging gospel into a new missiology that is in tune with an unpredictable, ever-changing cultural context.

# REFLECTIONS ON MULTICULTURAL LEADERSHIP

Lisa Anderson Umaña, El Salvador

"Pide perdón." "Ask forgiveness."

"Why?" retorted Evelyn.

"For arriving late to the staff meeting."

When that took place, I had already worked in Latin America for ten years so I was well aware of the Latin view of time and punctuality. But I was bound and determined that things would be run differently here in El Salvador. By insisting that latecomers make a public apology, I would create a different subculture here, similar to the one I had admired from a camp in the United States.

All but one of the tardy leaders subjected themselves to my humiliating request and entered the room with an apology.

Evelyn did not. She remained outside.

Later that week, we had another staff meeting. But this time it was I who asked forgiveness, thanks to the forthright confrontation of the Salvadorians and their natural resistance to "Yankee imperialism"—which is how they viewed my insistence on apologizing for being late. I count as one of my most loyal friends and coleaders that same Evelyn who remained outside the room.

Nothing is as ineffective as a foreigner who comes and tells Latins how things should be done. The prominent role North America has played in influencing its southern neighbors in modern times, as well as the historic antecedent of having been conquered by the Spaniards, may give Latins the propensities to either fight back or submit to outside influences. Humility would suggest that our leadership development processes and practices be rooted and responsive to the context and people. This type of humility has been sorely lacking in many of my efforts to develop leaders in Christian camping in Latin America.

For me, this part of the story is still in process. Although I have lived and worked in Latin America for almost twenty-five years, at times I feel like I am still wandering in the desert with regard to

crosscultural cues of how to form leaders who also form other leaders. I am learning not to fear the feeling of being lost and not having all the answers as I strengthen my relationship and trust in the
Pillar of Light who guides us by day and by night.

# PART III

# CONTEXTUALIZING LEADERSHIP

PART THREE DEALS WITH THE PROBLEM of how universal biblical truth intersects with diverse cultural values. It describes a model for integrating theology with leadership theory. While the Bible stipulates the ultimate purpose of leadership and a core understanding of the nature of reality, it does not prescribe leadership style. Though the Bible is our final authority, I suspect that God smiles at most of our cultural differences.

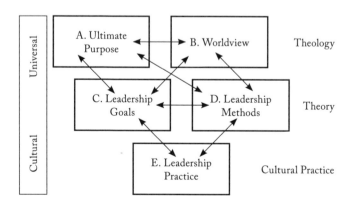

Figure III.1. Model of crosscultural leadership

The key tension of contextualization is the relationship between the universal absolutes of Scripture and the peculiarities of cultural differences. But the tension can be creative and fruitful. An overemphasis on absolutes leads to irrelevant application, while an overemphasis on culture can lead to relativistic absurdity.

In the next section we will explore a model that can facilitate working through the dilemma between biblical theology and the cultural practice of leadership.

# A THEOLOGY OF LEADERSHIP

*I do not think I am in the least inferior to those "super-apostles."*
*I have become all things to all people so that*
*by all possible means I might save some.*

THE APOSTLE PAUL WRITING TO THE CORINTHIANS

WHEN I SERVED AS A MISSIONARY I REPORTED to the Nigerian general secretary as well as to a North American SIM field director. It took me a while to learn the differences in their leadership styles. I know I made a lot of cultural blunders. I was most comfortable with an American style but wanted to adapt to Nigerian expectations. When we first arrived in Nigeria I instinctively called my low-power-distance American director "Bill" but I assumed my high-power-distance Nigerian supervisor should be called Rev. Kato. When I met with high-context Rev. Kato, I began by asking how he spent the night and if his family was well. He would do the same with me. Eventually we would get to the task at hand. In collectivistic societies it is important to build relationships before addressing the agenda. When I reported to my low-context SIM supervisor, we quickly got to my list of questions. I scheduled appointments with Bill, but felt free to just drop by the home or office of Rev. Kato. I reported to both of them, but I tried to adapt my "followership style" according to their leadership preferences. One of my happiest moments came when Rev. Kato called me "Jim" and urged me to call him "Byang." He was intentionally adapting to my comfort style. We became good friends, and I'll always be thankful for the brief years we enjoyed together until his untimely death at age thirty-seven. This book is dedicated to his memory.

Multicultural leaders must be flexible, able to shift their leadership approach according to expectations of the situation. They must not only be proficient in several leadership models, but must also learn to work comfortably *under* leaders with very different cultural expectations of followers. Missionaries from Korea must adapt their leadership expectations as they serve under Nigerian leaders. Nigerian missionaries sent to North America need to be aware of leadership differences as they work with pastors in the United States, and missionaries from the United States need to be flexible as they report to executives in the Bolivian church. Whether missionaries work with a totally unreached people group, team up with missionaries from several nations, teach in leadership training institutions, or serve under local leaders, they must learn to modify leadership styles in the same way they learn new languages. We live in a wonderful and potentially frustrating new world of crosscultural situational leadership.

## SITUATIONAL LEADERSHIP

Paul Hersey and Kenneth Blanchard popularized the idea of situational leadership, a concept that significantly changed perspectives on management.[1] Their basic point is that effective leaders are those who are able to *assess* followers for their level of interest, competency, maturity and motivation, and *adapt* their leadership style accordingly. For example, if subordinates don't understand their job, the effective leader will use a *telling* or directive style. When followers are moderately competent and somewhat motivated, the leader will switch to a *selling* style by explaining decisions. If employees are gaining in competency but are still a bit insecure, the effective leader will use a *participative* style with shared decision making. For the follower who is able, willing and confident, the leader lets go by fully *delegating* and wholly turning over responsibility.

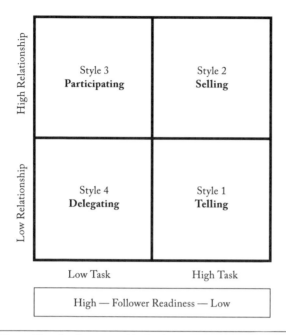

**Figure 9.1. Hersey Blanchard situational leadership**

## MULTICULTURAL SITUATIONAL LEADERSHIP

Multicultural situational leadership (fig. 9.2) will look somewhat different from the Hersey and Blanchard model (fig. 9.1). Effective leaders will be flexible in their style by assessing the *cultural* expectations of leaders and followers. As the cultural situation changes so does the leadership style. Effective multicultural followers will also adapt their understanding and expectations as they serve under leaders with different cultural expectations. Both leaders and followers must be aware of the expectations of the host culture, adapting accordingly. Multicultural leaders and followers need to be proficient in a wide range of leadership styles, and know when to use which one.

As churches and missions from around the world partner with each other, cultural flexibility is necessary for both leaders and followers. The following model has helped me think about flexibility. Unlike the Hersey Blanchard model, there is no sequence. The effective multicultural leader will seek to assess leadership expectations and adapt accordingly.

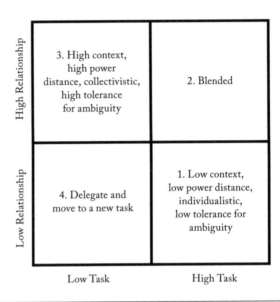

Figure 9.2. Multicultural situational leadersip

While figure 9.2 may oversimplify cultural variables, research and experience indicate that low-context cultures tend to be more task oriented while high-context cultures place a higher value on relationships. As a missionary in Nigeria, most of my leadership mistakes resulted from a mismatch between how the Nigerian culture expected me to lead and my own cultural preference in leading. For example, my preferred leadership style is low context with a low tolerance for ambiguity, but I served in a high-context culture that has a high tolerance for ambiguity. I was often task oriented and didn't pay enough attention to relationships. Rather than beginning a board meeting by asking each member for a short greeting and prayer update, I wanted to start on time and get on with the agenda. I remember offending a very important Nigerian board member and major donor by beginning the meeting "on time," rather than waiting for him to arrive. I embarrassed the recording secretary by publicly challenging his lack of accuracy in recording the minutes. I eventually learned to shift my leadership style from low to high context, and learned that relationships are more important than accomplishing precise tasks.

The model in figure 9.2 is also useful for the variables of power distance, individualism/collectivism, and tolerance for ambiguity. I wonder if high-context cultures place value on high power distance, collectivism, a tolerance for ambiguity, and a greater concern for interpersonal relationships. I suspect that low-context cultures generally prefer low power distance, value individual freedom, seek to avoid uncertainty and are more task-oriented. The model gives insights into how leaders and followers can be flexible. We lead and follow from the expectations of the other culture, rather than the values from our own upbringing.

How should leadership styles be adjusted? In high-power-distance cultures, loyalty may be more valued than competency. In collectivistic cultures, group harmony may be more important than praising someone for his or her individual achievement. Individual congratulations could threaten group cohesion and ostracize the person being praised. In societies with a low tolerance for ambiguity, goals will likely be precise, measurable and conform to a definite timetable. But where ambiguity is tolerated, such goals may be offensive.

## CULTURAL RELATIVISM

Many Christians would rightly critique the situational model as potentially leading to cultural relativism. "Just because something is cultural doesn't mean it is good." "Aren't bad leadership practices found in every culture?" "Don't we believe in biblical absolutes that challenge every culture?" So, how can crosscultural leaders be culturally relevant without being relativistic?

Biblical absolutes influence the multicultural practice of leadership, but too often leaders assume their limited culture-bound assumptions about leadership are both biblical and universal. When I served in Nigeria I remember listening to a visiting "expert" from the United States who conducted an American-type seminar he titled "Biblical Leadership." But instead of carefully exploring "the biblically absolute model of leadership," he was merely proof-texting his cultural biases. His naive myopic view of culture led to inappropriate teaching on leadership in Nigeria. How does one know the difference between valid cultural differences and biblical absolutes? Certainly there are biblical absolutes, but we must look at all of Scripture through the eyes of several cultures. The apostle Paul struggled with the same issue.

## PAUL IN CORINTH

Leadership conflicts were a major problem for the church in Corinth. The apostle Paul did not adapt to the culture when he chided the church about its leadership struggles.

> Brothers and sisters, I could not address you as spiritual but as worldly— mere infants in Christ. . . . For since there is jealousy and quarreling among you, are you not worldly? . . . For when one says, "I follow Paul," and another, "I follow Apollos," are you not mere human beings? . . .
>
> So neither the one who plants nor the one who waters is anything, but only God, who makes things grow. (1 Cor 3:1, 3-4, 7)

The churches in Corinth had the cultural expectation that effective leaders should be powerful, charismatic speakers. Paul warned the church about the dangers of this culturally accepted leadership style. He accused these so-called super-apostles of being "false apostles, deceitful workers, masquerading as apostles of Christ. And no wonder, for Satan himself masquerades as an angel of light" (2 Cor 11:13-14). There is no hint of cultural relativism in this passage.

It is amazing that the same apostle Paul, who boldly and dogmatically condemned leadership factions and false apostles, wrote this about his own leadership style: "I have become all things to all people so that by all possible means I might save some" (1 Cor 9:22). In the same chapter where he defends his leadership rights as an apostle, Paul claims a situational style: "I have made myself a slave to everyone, to win as many as possible" (1 Cor 9:19). It seems that at times his leadership values were based on biblical absolutes and at other times they were flexible, depending on whether he was dealing with the Jewish or Gentile culture. Biblical leaders must learn to live with the paradox of cultural relevance without cultural relativism. In order to know how to live with this paradox we must look at foundational questions of theology.

When leading or following in another culture, we need to be aware of the leadership values of our own culture and then ascertain those of the host culture. As we study a theology of leadership we will find many universal principles that should be applied in any culture. At times biblical principles reinforce particular cultural values and at other times they conflict with those values. Cultural insights describe what the leadership values *are*, but theology tells us what they *should* be. Too often we fall prey to the *naturalistic fallacy* that says the way things *are* is the way they *should* be. Christian theology places the authority of the Bible above culture. In order to distinguish the *is* from the *ought* we must look more deeply at a theology of leadership.

## THEOLOGY OF LEADERSHIP

How does a leader know when to be unbending and when to be situational? What are the supracultural absolutes regarding leadership? Let us look at fundamental questions that integrate theology with the theory and the practice of leadership.[2] We will look at theology from the traditional Christian perspective that assumes the Bible is given by God, is reliable and is the final authority. Here are the five interdependent foundational questions about leadership.

1. What is the ultimate purpose of leadership? Why does leadership exist?

2. What is the worldview of leadership? What are the assumptions about the nature of reality that influence leadership?

3. What are the goals of leadership? Growing out of the ultimate purpose and the worldview, what are the instrumental outcomes of leadership?

4. What are the methods of leadership? In light of an understanding of the ultimate purpose and worldview, how do leaders accomplish their task?

5. What does leadership look like in concrete practice? As a result of the above questions, what should the actual practice of leadership look like in the real world?

In this chapter we look closely at the ultimate purpose and world-view of leadership.

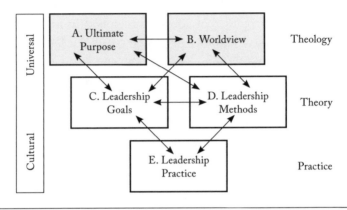

**Figure 9.3. Model of crosscultural leadership**

Here are some observations about the model:

- The ultimate purpose and worldview are primarily theological issues.

- We can learn a great deal about worldview from the natural and social sciences.

- From a biblical perspective, the ultimate purpose and worldview should be similar in every culture.

- Cultural differences are evident in the more specific question of leadership goals and methods.

- The ultimate purpose and goals of leadership (boxes A and C) are both types of leadership outcomes.

- Goals are more specific, but must contribute to the ultimate purpose.

- Goals and methods are theories of leadership and are modified by culture.

- The practice of leadership is the concrete outworking in the real world and is greatly influenced by culture.

One of my students suggested that we turn the model upside down and use the metaphor of an iceberg. The concrete practice of leadership is the tip of the iceberg and is the only aspect that is directly observable as it floats above the surface. We see examples of the concrete practice of leadership as we watch a Canadian youth pastor shepherding teenagers through customs at the airport, observe a Japanese pastor presiding over a committee meeting or see a Costa Rican missionary leading a discussion with youth in India. We can observe how they interact with others, how they use their hands to communicate, and what tone of voice they use. All this is box E. We can observe people as they lead, but we can only deduce their theories of leadership. Just as 90 percent of an iceberg is below the surface, so 90 percent of leadership is out of sight. The deeper theoretical questions of leadership goals and methods can be inferred by observation, but can't be seen directly. Even deeper below the surface are beliefs about the ultimate purpose and nature of leadership.

The model helps multicultural leaders integrate supracultural biblical absolutes with local cultural variability. Let's look at the first two questions in more detail.

### BOX A: THE ULTIMATE PURPOSE OF LEADERSHIP

Every culture and organization has an assumed ultimate purpose for leaders. People don't stop to think about purposes, but everyone subconsciously knows what they are. Different societies expect their leaders to promote freedom for the individual, the happiness of the family, the survival of the community or the economic growth of a nation. People expect politicians to provide security and prosperity. Churchgoers expect pastors to meet their needs. The ultimate purpose of the typical corporate chief executive officer is to increase the value of the company and provide wealth for shareholders.

As Christians, our primary source of knowledge about the ultimate purpose of leadership is the Bible. It ties in with assumptions about the ultimate purpose of life. Why do human beings exist? Why did God make us? Godly leadership exists to promote God's ultimate purpose for the individual, the world and himself. Scripture states this purpose in several ways.

- *Know God.* The heart-cry and ultimate purpose of the apostle Paul was to know Christ. By *knowing,* he meant having a deep intimate relationship. He writes,

  > But whatever were gains to me I now consider loss for the sake of Christ. What is more, I consider everything a loss because of the surpassing worth of *knowing* Christ Jesus my Lord, for whose sake I have lost all things. I consider them garbage, that I may gain Christ. . . . I want to *know* Christ—yes, to know the power of his resurrection and participation in his sufferings, becoming like him in his death, and so, somehow, attaining to the resurrection from the dead. (Phil 3:7-8, 10-11, italics added)

- *Glorify God.* The psalmist announces, "Glorify the LORD with me; let us exalt his name together" (Ps 34:3). Again and again the Bible proclaims that we exist not for our own comfort or happiness but for the glory of God. "To him be glory in the church and in Christ Jesus throughout all generations, for ever and ever! Amen" (Eph 3:21). We will spend eternity acclaiming, "Amen! Praise and glory and wisdom and thanks and honor and power and strength be to our God for ever and ever. Amen!" (Rev 7:12; see also Rev 15:3-4; 19:6-8).

- *Love God.* When Jesus was asked which was the greatest commandment he quoted Moses: "'Love the Lord your God with all your heart and with all your soul and with all your mind.' This is the first and greatest commandment" (Mt 22:37-38; Deut 6:5; see also Deut 10:12). This is the ultimate command of both the Old and New Testaments.

- *Fear God.* Seldom do we find "the fear of the Lord" in organizational mission statements, yet this is a constant biblical theme. Even as Moses commands Israel to love the Lord, he also instructs them to "fear the LORD your God as long as you live" (Deut 6:2). "Fear the LORD your God, serve him only and take your oaths in his name" (Deut 6:13). "What does the LORD your God ask of you but to fear the LORD your God" (Deut 10:12; see also Deut 31:12-13). The apostle Paul wrote, "Since, then, we know what it is to fear the Lord, we try to persuade people" (2 Cor 5:11).

The ultimate purpose of leadership is to bring people into full relationship with their Creator. We are created to know, love and glorify God. These purposes are not only ultimate but eternal; we exist to praise God for ever and ever. To know, glorify, love and fear God is not only our ultimate purpose, but our highest motivation.

It is common for Christian organizations to include "the glory of God" in their purpose statements, but this is often ignored in daily thinking. I recently heard a mission executive make fun of the purpose statements of most Christian organizations by cynically mimicking, "Our purpose is to glorify God, blah, blah, blah." The phrase is taken for granted and becomes a meaningless prelude to the real goals of the organization. This is dangerous.

Other values unobtrusively slip into box A. We say we exist to glorify God, but in fact, our primary concern is to grow church membership, increase the number of missionaries, distribute more Christian DVDs or have more programs. When the organization faces a crisis, the ultimate purpose becomes survival. As we struggle to make decisions we tend to ask, Is this good for me? or Is this good for the organization? We should be asking, Is this good for the kingdom of God? Our passion for knowing and loving God must be so overwhelming that we are willing to sacrifice ourselves and our organizations for the sake of his glory.

Knowing, glorifying and loving God are difficult to quantify, so we seldom include them in the evaluation process. We are tempted to evaluate goals that are easy to measure but that are much less significant. The final evaluation of leadership and of organizations is to ask, Did our efforts, programs, finances, structures and leadership style bring glory to God? Did these help people to know and love God? Too often we merely ask, Did the organization grow under my leadership? Did the budget increase? Did we plant more churches? Instead we must ask, Did the budget make God glad? Do people in the churches we planted truly love God more deeply? The fact that we will never be able to precisely quantify and evaluate the ultimate purpose must not dissuade us from being passionate about God's glory. The Lord will likely give us glimpses or indications of leadership effectiveness, but most of the critical outcomes will only be known in eternity.

## BOX B: THE WORLDVIEW OF LEADERSHIP

Both leaders and followers have assumptions about the nature of reality, and these assumptions greatly influence why and how we lead. The worldview of a leader is formed through assumptions about the nature of reality. Christian worldview assumptions, which are valid across all cultures, include these:

1. *There is a God who created us, loves us and has a purpose for us.* People were created to have fellowship with their Creator. The ultimate purpose of the leader is to be an instrument of God to facilitate this purpose. God is the only ultimate leader, while human leaders exist to serve him. Human leaders, no matter how powerful or gifted, must be humble before their Creator. There is no room for arrogance in any human leader.

2. *Satan is real and wants to destroy God's plan and his people.* We are not on a mechanical assembly line, where the leader is in control of the process or the outcome. We are in a battle, not against flesh and blood, but against powers of this dark world, against spiritual forces of evil (Eph 6:12). Leaders must expect opposition, discouragement and challenges. We can only succeed when we are covered by the full armor of God.

3. *God created a real world that has a beginning and will have an end.* Godly leadership is needed in every aspect of God's creation—in business, politics, the home, professions and the sciences. The fact that the world has a beginning and an end makes progress possible. We can be used of God to make a better world, build the church and care for the environment. The fact that the world is not an illusion and that progress is possible is not a common assumption in some world religious systems.

4. *The Bible is God's primary communication to human beings.* In many societies the king is law and ethics are situational. For the Christian, God is king and his law is absolute. The Bible is universally true and authoritative for every culture. This means that leaders in every society are held accountable to God's Word.

5. *Human beings are created in the image of God and will live forever.* If the ultimate purpose of leadership is to bring glory to God, the primary

goal of leadership is to facilitate the development of people so they become all God created them to be. The atheistic philosophy contends that people are expendable for the sake of the government. Christian theology argues that governments come and go, but people live forever. People are more important than institutions, including the organizations we lead.

6. *All humans are fallen creatures with natural tendencies for evil.* Christians are not surprised that "power tends to corrupt, and absolute power corrupts absolutely. Great men are almost always bad men."[3] Even the most godly leaders in any culture must be deathly afraid of pride. The Bible shows very few examples of consistent godly leadership. Because of the Fall, there must be limits to power. Checks and balances are essential. Godly leaders help to limit the effects of evil in followers. The darkest days in Israel were during the absence of judges, when everyone did what was right in their own eyes. Both leaders and followers have a natural tendency toward evil.

7. *God sent Jesus into the world to redeem us and demonstrate godly leadership.* We are created in the image of God with great worth, but we are also fallen and rebellious against our Creator. The solution to this dilemma is Jesus, the Son of God, who died for our sins to reconcile us to God and one another. All the problems in the world are directly or indirectly caused by sin, and Jesus is the only solution to the sin problem. Poverty, war, greed, oppression and sickness are the result of the fallen world, so the most competent leader in the world cannot solve any major problem without the gospel of Jesus. The goal of leadership is to point people to Jesus. Jesus is also the example of the ideal leader: "For even the Son of Man did not come to be served, but to serve, and to give his life as a ransom for many" (Mk 10:45). The idea of a servant leader is astounding and universally countercultural.[4]

8. *The Holy Spirit empowers believers and gives spiritual gifts to all who know him.* As Jesus prepared his disciples for his ascension into heaven, he promised an Advocate, the Holy Spirit, who would be with the disciples and in them (Jn 14:15-27). He told his disciples to wait for the gift promised by the Father. They would not be witnesses until they received power when the Holy Spirit came on them (Acts 1:4, 8). Lead-

ership without the Holy Spirit is powerless and useless. The Holy Spirit gives gifts to all believers. These spiritual gifts are not given for our self-actualization, but to build up the body of Christ. One legitimate definition of leadership is the ability to *influence* others. In this important sense, all believers are called to be influencers, using gifts for the sake of the church.

9. *God intends believers to grow into the fullness of the stature of Christ.* Christians must grow. Paul reminds us in Ephesians that the purpose of spiritual gifts is "so that the body of Christ may be built up until we all reach unity in the faith . . . and become mature, attaining to the whole measure of the fullness of Christ" (Eph 4:12-13). The leadership goal of apostles, prophets, evangelists, pastors and teachers is to equip gifted believers to build up the body of Christ so that individuals may be mature in Christ. The task is both collectivistic *(the body of Christ)* and individualistic *(so that each person may be mature in Christ)*. Leaders are developmentalists, as they seek to develop the community and the individual. All other agendas must be subservient to this.

10. *The church—the body of Christ—is a necessary means for Christians to grow in Christ.* "From him the whole body, joined and held together by every supporting ligament, grows and builds itself up in love, as each part does its work" (Eph 4:16). Spiritually gifted leaders cannot grow as leaders without the rest of the body of Christ. One biblical metaphor for the church is a *kingdom of priests* (see Ex 19:6; 1 Pet 2:5, 9; Rev 5:10). This doctrine of the priesthood of all believers was not unique to the Reformers—they merely rediscovered a major teaching of all of Scripture. This doctrine has astounding implications for a theology of leadership.

11. *Jesus is coming again to judge the world.* Paul preached to the Athenians, "For he has set a day when he will judge the world with justice by the man he has appointed. He has given proof of this to everyone by raising him from the dead" (Acts 17:31). Jesus is coming again, this time as Lord and King. Leaders often attempt to evaluate the success of their programs. But the ultimate evaluation of ministry effectiveness will not be measured by popular acclaim. We wait for our Father's words: "Well done, good and faithful servant." While God may encourage us with hints of success here, our final evaluation will not be

fully realized in this world. My mother posted a poem in our kitchen that read, "Only one life, will soon be past; Only what's done for Christ will last."

12. *People will live forever in heaven or hell.* God loved the world so much that he sent his Son, so that those who believe in him should not perish, but have eternal life (Jn 3:16). This assumption has huge implications for leaders. People have infinite, eternal worth. Leaders who strive to meet physical and social needs without evangelism are missing an eternal dimension. Servant leaders who love the people they serve will seek to meet physical and social needs as well as spiritual needs. Because people will outlive their bodies, concern for temporal needs is not enough. Heaven is more glorious than anything we can envision. All our hopes, dreams and longings will be perfectly fulfilled there. With unimaginable joy, we will be able to realize our ultimate purpose of knowing and loving God. I suspect hell will be a place where God gives people freedom to be themselves, without his grace.

The purpose and the worldview of leadership are intertwined. A bad theology of leadership will inevitably result in bad leaders. Leadership grounded in God's glory and driven by a scriptural worldview is the hope of the global church.

# REFLECTIONS ON
# MULTICULTURAL LEADERSHIP

Valentine Kwame Hayibor, Ghana

I grew up in Ghana with a high communal orientation to life. I discovered that the web of relationships, including the traditional family, were critical in shaping my personal leadership style and behavior. Both the nuclear and extended family were important transmitters of culture which eventually influenced my leadership perceptions and attitude. Yet I have also been exposed to cultures that emphasize individuality and that influenced my personal leadership development. Even so, God has allowed me to see the bigger picture of a shared journey where he has used others to help me gain perspective, renewal and empowerment. This took place through exposure to mentors, counsel, encouragement and inspiration. I have found that growth opportunities take place when an emerging leader commits himself to valuing the differences that each leadership or cultural environment brings to his development process.

When I turned twelve, my parents enrolled me in a boarding school—a Catholic minor seminary run exclusively by missionaries from a multicultural context—Britain, France, Germany, Canada and the United States. I spent six remarkable years (five years as a student and one year on staff) in this cultural environment. The influence of this devout multicultural missionary team prompted my desire to think as well as act crossculturally. Vincent Kerr, from Ireland, particularly took me under his mentorship and taught me public debating, social ethics and the desire to be an advocate for the physically challenged in society. I came to an initial appreciation that the task of leadership in a multicultural context is to weave a tapestry of relationships that recognizes the nuances in cultures while fostering bridges of understanding. It was immensely useful to accept one's perceptions of "others" without uncharitable judgments.

My subsequent experiences as the national director of Ghana Campus Crusade for Christ, a mission organization with a relatively American-centric work ethic, along with opportunities to travel in over twenty countries, have sharpened my skills in valuing the differences that each person brings to the leadership setting.

At Trinity Evangelical Divinity School, where I am working on a doctoral degree in intercultural studies, one of the professors, the late Dr. Paul Hiebert, had a profound influence on my leadership paradigm. He remarked in one of his last statements to a group of international students: "Remember, God is writing his story in your lives." I believe this should be the trajectory and essence of my leadership in any culture—an opportunity to be transformed from within and to help transform society.

# A THEORY OF LEADERSHIP

*There is nothing as practical as good theory or as useless as bad theory.*

EDWIN P. PLUEDDEMANN, RESEARCH SCIENTIST

THE RESEARCH CHEMISTS IN MY DAD'S LAB gave him a T-shirt emblazoned with "Iconoclast." I wasn't sure if it was intended as a compliment or a criticism. I looked up the word and discovered that iconoclasts don't live according to the cherished beliefs of the institution. Apparently Dad didn't fit the mold or the expectations of company management. Interestingly, the year he was inducted into the Plastics Hall of Fame[1] was the same year he received the lowest rating from his manager. It seems that he didn't have his chemicals well organized and there was dust on his lab equipment. But his worst offense was that he resisted setting goals. When his manager asked him to state his work objectives for the year, he grinned and said that he intended to play with his chemistry set and discover revolutionary molecular theories. Dad's creative approach earned him a hundred patents before he died.

Inventors don't set precise goals because they are solving unpredictable problems.[2] One evening while at the dinner table, my dad received a phone call from the scientists at Cape Canaveral. They were having difficulty sticking the ceramic heat-shield tiles to the space shuttle. Since he invented the glue that held them together, he gave them several suggestions and told them to call him in the morning. Sure enough, his suggestions worked. Solving unexpected problems with unpredictable solutions is a common leadership task.

When my dad came home from work he would tell us what he had discovered that day and would then exclaim, "There is nothing as practical as good theory." He had confidence that if he understood the theoretical structure of molecules he could solve any problem. General Motors might phone him with a problem about how to prevent water from leaking in around the windshield, or IBM might query him about stronger lamination on circuit boards. A sporting manufacturer would ask for help in improving fiberglass fishing poles, or the Army would ask him how to stick the nose cone on the Patriot missile. His understanding of coupling-agent theories prepared him to make varied practical discoveries.

Dad had a biblical worldview. His scientific discoveries grew out of his conviction that God had created a rational universe with consistent laws. I remember one morning asking him what he was going to do that day. He told me he pictured God looking over the battlements of heaven to see if scientists like himself could discover how he had designed molecules. Because he was convinced that God was in control of the universe, he could live with ambiguity in his research. His *theological* worldview informed his scientific *theory*, which in turn influenced his research *practice*.

### WHY THEORY?

Missionaries pride themselves in being practical people. For many, if something is "theoretical" it is impractical. Yet every leader relies on some kind of theory, either explicit or implicit. I agree with my dad that nothing is as practical as good theory, and nothing is more impractical than bad theory. In fact, unexamined theory can be dangerous.

What is theory? It is a mental picture of why things work the way they do. Some theories are elegant and well tested, such as Einstein's theory of relativity. They help explain why the world works the way it does. Other theories are informal guesses. I knew a man who thought he could predict the weather by the level of pain in his knee. If his knee hurt, he knew it was going to rain.

There are many unfortunate stories of missionaries who have held to unexamined theories of leadership. I remember a North American builder who came to supervise the construction of a Nigerian Bible college. He assumed that building a classroom would be the same in any culture. Without reflecting on the underlying cultural theories, he began to set precise job targets and completion dates. He became frustrated when the building materials didn't arrive on the promised day. He attempted to motivate the laborers by paying them individually according to how many cement blocks they laid. The strategy backfired when the laborers refused to compete with their brothers and cousins. His frustration grew into anger. He went back to the United States telling hurtful stories about people who wouldn't work hard and couldn't plan ahead. The local people were glad to see him go and figured out how to build the classroom on their own. A conflict of underlying cultural assumptions undercut his leadership. He assumed that everyone in the world came from an individualistic culture with a low tolerance for ambiguity. He didn't have a clue how to work with people in a collectivistic society with a high tolerance for ambiguity. An unexamined theory of leadership is dangerous.

## INTEGRATING THEORY WITH THE THEOLOGY AND PRACTICE OF LEADERSHIP

In this chapter we will look at the task and the methods of leadership. These should grow out of theological assumptions about the ultimate purpose and worldview, and then be reflected in leadership practice. While most ministry leaders hold to a biblical theology, too often their theory of leadership comes from popular books that run counter to good theology. It is dangerous to lose the connection between the theory and theology of leadership. Let's look again at the big-picture model of crosscultural leadership.

I expect that most Christian leaders around the world hold to similar beliefs regarding the theology of ultimate purpose and worldview. Theo-

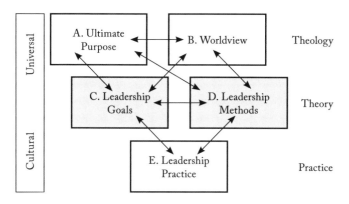

Figure 10.1. Model of crosscultural leadership

ries about the task and methods of leadership are more culturally attuned and will look slightly different in every culture. The actual practice of leadership is deeply embedded in the cultural context and will vary greatly.

The interrelationship among theology, theory and practice is cyclical (fig. 10.2). Excellent leadership theory must grow out of good theology and be echoed in the actual practice of leadership. The practice of leadership must be evaluated by how it contributes to the ultimate purpose and how it reflects a biblical worldview of leadership.

Even though leadership will look different in every culture, the underlying description of the leader will be fundamentally the same in every culture.

*Good leaders are fervent disciples of Jesus Christ, gifted by the Holy Spirit, with a passion to bring glory to God. They use their gift of leadership by taking initiative to focus, harmonize and enhance the gifts of others for the sake of developing people and cultivating the kingdom of God.*

This description grows out of the ultimate purpose of leadership: to bring glory to God and to help others to know, love and fear him. It also takes into account theological assumptions about the nature of reality, or the worldview of leadership. God made us for himself, and people have immeasurable eternal value. Yet we are fallen creatures, needing redemption. We live in a world created by God yet influenced by evil. Humans are created with the amazing developmental potential to grow into the likeness of Christ. The body of Christ is the environ-

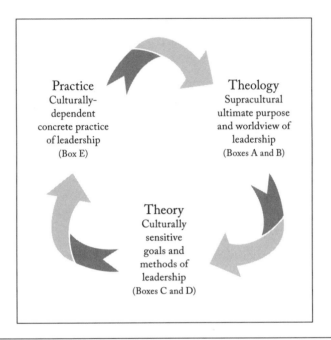

Practice
Culturally-
dependent
concrete practice
of leadership
(Box E)

Theology
Supracultural
ultimate purpose
and worldview of
leadership
(Boxes A and B)

Theory
Culturally
sensitive
goals and
methods of
leadership
(Boxes C and D)

Figure 10.2

ment for nurture, and the Holy Spirit gives spiritual gifts to be used to influence one another toward Christlikeness.

## BOX C: GOALS OF LEADERSHIP

What do leaders do? What do they hope to accomplish? What is their mission? The fundamental purpose of leadership is to glorify God by facilitating the development of people. This is the criteria for evaluating the effectiveness of leaders. When we stand before the throne of

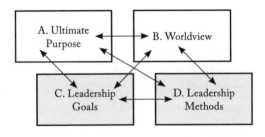

Figure 10.3

Christ we will not be judged for how busy we've been or how many good things we've accomplished. We will be evaluated by how much we have loved Christ and how much we have influenced others to love, know, glorify and fear him. The greatest command is not to plant megachurches, found a global ministry or be an outstanding Bible translator. The greatest command is to love the Lord our God with all our heart, soul, mind and strength.

The goals of leadership must grow out of the ultimate purpose and will reflect the worldview of the leader.

***Leadership is a gift of the Spirit.*** Leadership is a gift, whether distinctly Christian or secular. In Romans 13 we read that all governing authorities are established by God and are God's servants (Rom 13:1-4). Earlier in the book I make the case that leadership is influence, and that all believers are given spiritual gifts to influence the body of Christ. In a real sense, then, all believers are leaders. Spiritual gifts are given for the common good, not merely for individual self-actualization (1 Cor 12:7).

Nevertheless, one of the gifts mentioned in Romans 12 is the gift of leadership.[3] If all believers are leaders, how can there be a special gift of leadership? And aren't apostles and teachers leaders as well? Several translations note that the word for leadership can also mean "to provide for others" or "to give aid." It seems that while all believers have spiritual gifts to be used in roles of leadership, there is a special gift that is intended to be used to coordinate the gifts of others. Thus, there are two types of leaders. First, all believers have spiritual gifts to lead or influence the body of Christ. Second, some leaders have a specialized gift to focus, harmonize and coordinate the giftedness of other believers. All believers are leaders in the first sense, and many have the potential to grow into the second kind of leader.

At times missionaries have held on to positions of leadership for too long, complaining that the newly planted church doesn't have any leaders. Since leadership is a gift, we are assured that the Holy Spirit gives this gift wherever and whenever it is needed. If we say that a body of believers doesn't have any leaders, are we really saying that the Holy Spirit has failed to do his work? Spiritually gifted leaders often don't fit our stereotype of an ideal leader. They seldom have flamboyant personalities with formal theological credentials. Leadership is a gift of the Spirit, and the task of the leader-developer is to fan into flame the gift God has already given (2 Tim 1:6).

Since leadership is a gift of the Spirit, it is available to both men and women. Spiritual gifts are not gender specific. Women then should not only be allowed to take leadership roles, but they should be urged to do so. I'm convinced that, properly understood, the Bible does not contradict itself. So when the apostle Paul instructs women in Ephesus to keep silent (1 Tim 2:12), then tells Corinthian women to pray and prophesy with covered heads (1 Cor 11:5), he is giving different guidelines for different cultural situations.[4] It is because of my high view of the plenary inspiration of Scripture that I believe that women should be encouraged to use their God-given gifts of leadership.

Though the role of women in leadership is not limited by universal biblical principles, it is influenced by cultural situations. There will be some situations where it would not be appropriate for women to take on a position of formal leadership, and the same principle would apply to men. For example, in a Muslim context it would not be appropriate for men to assume leadership for a women's Bible study.[5]

*Leaders bring glory to God.* We need to be reminded often that leaders don't exist to bring glory to themselves, their churches, their mission agencies or their projects. The glory is for God alone. Possibly the greatest temptation for leaders is to turn a secondary task into the ultimate one. The leadership task grows directly out of the ultimate purpose of leadership. Everything a leader does must contribute to the glory of God.

*The leader takes initiative.* Leaders make decisions. How they make decisions depends on cultural expectations and the situation. They may consult first and then make a decision, or they may decide to delegate the decision to others. In a time of crisis a decision may be made with very little consultation. Leaders may be deeply involved in the *process* of decision making while entrusting the actual decision to others. How leaders take initiative may take many forms, but all leaders take initiative.

Leaders face the danger of two extremes: being an autocratic dictator or a do-nothing laissez-faire doormat. The autocrat ignores the giftedness of others and the prideful dangers of our fallen nature. The laissez-faire doormat doesn't lead, ignoring the danger of "everyone doing what is right in their own eyes." Autocratic leaders control the final decision, as well as the decision-making process. Laissez-faire leaders don't influence either the decision or the decision-making process. Too often leadership is either autocratic or laissez faire. There is another possibility—a consultative approach. Most often, effective leaders take proactive initiative to influence the *process* of decision making, and together with others, make the final decision through consensus.

In times of crisis I have occasionally used an autocratic style. When my best friend was killed in an airplane crash in Nigeria, I organized ground and air search parties without much consultation. Looking back, I'm surprised at how autocratic I was and how people did what I told them to do.

There are times when the laissez-faire approach is best. After I turned over the directorship of the ECWA Christian Education Department to my Nigerian colleague Samuila Kure, I cheered him on, but was not involved in either the leadership process or outcomes of the department. He did a much better job without me looking over his shoulder.

Most often, though, I prefer the consultative approach. I remember when we as a mission wrestled with setting up a brand new financial support system. I took initiative in calling groups together and outlining the problem we needed to solve, but I trusted the wisdom of a multitude of counselors when it came to making final decisions. I was proactive in the process, but trusted people smarter than myself with the end product.

During my time as international director of SIM, a multicultural missionary team in South America had difficulty working toward a coordinated vision and strategy. The team was in shambles, with several missionaries working in isolation and others working in competition with each other. Interteam tensions were growing. I took initiative by traveling to South America and called for a week-long team retreat. After listening to each member of the team describe the situation, I summarized what they already knew. "The team is not effective. You are not helping each other. In fact, at times you are hindering each other's ministries. I don't think this is what the Lord intends. What do

|  | Leader controls the *decision* | Leader does **not** control the *decision* |
|---|---|---|
| Leader Proactively influences the decision *process* | Autocratic | Consultative |
| Leader does **not** control the decision *process* | Manipulative | Laissez Faire |

**Figure 10.4**

you suggest?" After a couple days of sharing personal vision and praying for each other, they brainstormed ideas for revamping their strategy
and decided to meet again in six months. It took two additional meetings, but at the end of the year each member understood the personal
vision of each team member and hammered out a joint vision and strategy. At their own initiative, they quit one ministry in the north of the
country and strengthened one of their most productive ministries in
the south. Their changing consensus on vision led to a radical shift of
ministries. As the international director, I was heavy-handed with the
*process* of change, but set the stage for a consensus decision from within
the mission team.

   *Leaders harmonize the gifts of others.* When singers harmonize, all are
singing different notes. Choir directors lead the distinctive voices of many
people to make one beautiful sound. The bass doesn't have the gifts to be
an alto, and the soprano can reach notes not possible for a baritone. All

sing different notes, so that together they make a melodious sound. The most challenging leadership task is turning soloists into a choir.

The frustrating problem in the Corinthian church was lack of harmony. Paul wrote that the church was like a body—each member had an individual function, so that the whole body would work together in unity (1 Cor 12:12-31).

Like the Corinthian church, it seems that the natural tendency in the body of Christ around the world is disharmony. Collectivistic cultures place such a high value on harmony that they may hide destructive and divisive tensions. Individualistic cultures tend to glory in personal preferences and need special prodding to promote harmony. Leadership in multicultural situations is impossible without blended gifts. So before leaders can promote vision and strategy they must promote unified harmony.

God's solution to the disharmony in Corinth is seen in chapter 13. Leaders must stimulate team members to eagerly desire this greatest gift. "Love is patient, love is kind. It does not envy, it does not boast, it is not proud. It does not dishonor others, it is not self-seeking, it is not easily angered, it keeps no record of wrongs" (1 Cor 13:4-5). The task of the leader is to model, teach and pray for loving relationships.

*Leaders enhance the gifts of others.* Jesus preached the good news and healed the sick. He also spent much of his time enhancing the giftedness of his disciples. As the apostle Paul traveled, he planted churches and developed leaders. He helped Timothy to stir up the gift that was in him. The whole purpose of spiritual gifts is for the common good—to build up the church.

Ineffective leaders might accomplish great feats, yet destroy people in the process. The most basic task of leaders is to develop people for God's glory. Autocratic leaders accomplish tasks by using people as a mere means. This hinders the accomplishment of the deeper task—developing people. Laissez-faire leaders tend to be directionless, having little ability to develop people. God calls Christians to be salt and light in the world and to make disciples of all nations. Effective leaders don't use people to accomplish the job; instead they use the job to develop people. Successful leaders enhance the spiritual gifts of people by involving them in ministry.[6]

*Leaders focus the gifts of others.* One of the hardest tasks for leaders is to get the team pulling in the same direction. It's difficult for two horses to pull a wagon if they are pulling in opposite directions. The key is vision-driven teamwork.

I know of leaders who tried to dictate their personal vision to the rest of a multicultural team, only to be soundly rebuffed. I've also worked with talented and highly motivated missionaries with a common ministry focus. They helped each other and were highly effective.

A beautiful example of a leader who harmonized, enhanced and focused the giftedness of others was Dr. Aletta Bell, the SIM director for India. She delightfully turned the field upside down.

Our first official visit to India was discouraging. The field lacked leaders who could focus the gifts of others. The missionaries were disheartened and leaving the field. One missionary commented that the group's long-range vision was, "The last person leaving, turn the lights out."

Soon after the visit, I appointed seasoned medical doctor Aletta Bell to be the new field director. She was a contagious possibility thinker! She traveled from Canada to Australia and many places in between, proclaiming the opportunities in India. The Lord used her visionary leadership to recruit a multicultural team focused on vision-driven ministry. She developed younger missionaries by giving them administrative responsibility and mentoring them as leaders.

On our last trip to India, Carol and I were overjoyed to find young missionaries from about a dozen countries working together, effectively focused on ministry. On our final evening we met on the beach overlooking the Arabian Sea for a time of worship and singing. As the sun set over the ocean, someone put a music tape in the "boom box." Children lit sparklers, and team members from China, Guatemala, Canada, Japan and Ethiopia danced on the beach. We thank the Lord for the leadership gifts of Aletta Bell as she focused, enhanced and harmonized the gifts of young missionaries.

*Leaders help people grow into their full God-given potential.* The imperative task of leadership is facilitating the growth of others. This is much more important than what we normally think of as the leadership task. We often think of great leaders as presidents who build massive universities, generals who win glorious victories, or CEOs who multiply the value of the company by a thousandfold.

Bill Pollard has served as CEO of ServiceMaster and as chair of the Board of Trustees of Wheaton College. He writes, "If I were to summarize what I have often said about leadership, it would be that the real and lasting measurement of achievement is in the changed lives of the people being led."[7] Another dear friend who recently went to be with the Lord is Paul Gordon of Gordon Food Service. GFS is the largest privately held foodservice distributor in North America, with sales in 2007 of over five billion dollars. Paul was famous for his love for people and his desire for employees to have fulfilling lives. Christian leaders—whether in the church, in mission agencies or in the business arena—understand that their most critical task is to develop people.

Older leadership theory assumed that the work of leaders was to accomplish a task through people. The task was to make sales, build buildings, win elections, mobilize armies or mow the yard. People were seen as human resources rather than resourceful humans. But what if that formula is turned around? What if the real task is not primarily to accomplish work, but to develop people? *Effective leaders use the task to develop people.*

**Leaders help the body of Christ to become mature.** The core goal of leadership is to develop people—not just as individuals but in the body of Christ. This means incorporating the values of both individualist and collectivist cultures.

> Christ himself gave the apostles, the prophets, the evangelists, the pastors and teachers, to equip his people for works of service, so that the body of Christ may be built up until we all reach unity in the faith and in the knowledge of the Son of God and become mature, attaining to the whole measure of the fullness of Christ. (Eph 4:11-13)

Christ gave his people gifts of leadership so that both individuals and the body may become mature. The leadership task is to promote the transformation of the household of God into the measure of the fullness of Christ.

What does "the measure of fullness" look like? We can ask, Is the church as a body obedient to the word of God? Is the community reaching out to make disciples of all nations? Are believers becoming salt and light in their communities? Is the church transforming the world of business and politics? Do families in the church shine as light to a dark world?

## BOX D: LEADERSHIP METHODS

When people think about leadership, the first thing that comes to mind is technique. We continuously seek more efficient schemes. Instead we should ask, What is the most *effective* way to accomplish the task? Leadership methods are the means of fulfilling the task and must reflect theological convictions about the ultimate purpose and worldview.

Popular books on leadership are filled with methodological fads. I have a whole bookshelf dedicated to books on leadership methods that include total quality management, transactional techniques, management-by-walking-around and the one-minute manager. Some "interesting" books on technique include *The Leadership Secrets of Attila the Hun, Warrior Politics: Why Leadership Demands a Pagan Ethos,* and *The Contrarian's Guide to Leadership.*[8] *Jack: Straight from the Gut* describes the leadership methods of Jack Welch, including the strategy of firing the bottom 10 percent of leaders each year.[9] I have found these books to be fascinating and parts of them helpful. My point is that the majority of books on leadership, both Christian and secular, teach techniques on how to grow the organization, without taking the time to reflect on the eternal task of developing people.[10]

Some Christian books on leadership parrot the ideas of secular books and interject Bible verses to proof-text their point. It isn't difficult to find examples for any leadership method in the Bible. Should leaders crack the whip like Jesus did when chasing out the money-changers in the temple, or should they wash the feet of followers as Jesus did in the upper room? Focusing on methods divorced from theological reflection is hazardous.

## CULTURAL EXPECTATIONS

Cultures have different expectations for how leaders will behave. Charles Handy has written a helpful book about leadership metaphors titled *The Gods of Management*.[11] I have found the book helpful as I teach courses in crosscultural leadership with multicultural students. Students from diverse parts of the world resonate with the different mental images of leadership. The four leadership descriptions are based on Greek gods:

1. *Zeus* leaders are paternalistic father-figures. They act impulsively, think intuitively, value loyalty in followers and develop leaders through apprenticeships. Most Zeus leaders are benevolent, seeking the good of the family. Employees are treated like family members and are expected to be devoted to their leader. The cultural values of Zeus leaders are high context, collectivistic, high power distance, and they demonstrate a high tolerance for ambiguity.

2. *Apollo* is the god of order and rules. These leaders are the policy police officers. They love systems, job descriptions, thick manuals, organization charts, forms and precise standards. They value predictability and logical analysis. Such low-context leaders reflect the cultural values of individualism, high power distance and low tolerance for ambiguity.

3. *Athena* is the team coordinator of a commando unit. She is a problem solver—a proactive group leader with a consultative leadership style. She sees team members as "resourceful humans" rather than "human resources." She might fit the cultural values of collectivism, low power distance and high tolerance for ambiguity.

4. *Dionysus* is the individualist. The organization exists to make sure the individual achieves personal goals. Group members recognize no boss, but work with coordinators. In the Dionysian organization, each person has a veto over decisions. Individuals work in loose-knit partnerships that are convenient for them. (Handy suggests that most university professors and medical doctors are Dionysian.) They are highly individualistic, low power distance among themselves, and low context. I'm not sure where they fit on an ambiguity scale.

Fons Trompenaars and Charles Hampden-Turner suggest four similar metaphors that reflect national cultures.[12]

1. *The family culture* is hierarchical and personal. Relationships are face-to-face and power oriented. The company is a family with the responsibility of taking care of the needs of employees who are expected to be loyal and obedient. These cultures are high context, with a high value on collectivistic harmony, high power distance and a high tolerance for ambiguity. Japan, France and Spain are examples.

2. *The Eiffel Tower culture* is bureaucratic and hierarchical. Like the Eiffel Tower in Paris, it is narrow at the top and broad at the lower levels. The leader does not need to be personal. The role of the leader is more important than the personal qualities of the individual. The company values efficiency and the achievement of predetermined goals. Decisions are logical and follow the rules. The culture would be low context, individualistic and high power distance, with a low tolerance for ambiguity. German and Austrian companies are given as examples.

3. *The guided missile culture* is egalitarian and project-oriented. Leaders are coordinators of experts and are loyal to their profession rather than to each other or to the company. As soon as the specific task is finished, they may leave their coworkers and change to another company. These cultures would be low context, individualistic, low power distance and low tolerance for ambiguity. The United States and the United Kingdom are examples.

4. *The incubator culture* "is based on the existential idea that organizations are secondary to the fulfillment of individuals."[13] Companies are incubators for self-expression and self-fulfillment. They are both personal and egalitarian. Examples are small start-up companies in Silicon Valley, a legal firm, a medical practice or an artists group. Leadership is achieved by skill, not ascribed by position. The best artist or computer programmer becomes the leader. The culture is high context, low power distance and collectivistic, with a high tolerance for ambiguity. Sweden is an example.

Leaders use any number of methods or styles. They can be autocratic, democratic, directive, nondirective, participative or consultative.

The literature is replete with research on leadership methods. The GLOBE study includes charismatic, team-oriented, participative, humane-oriented, autonomous and self-protective.[14]

The methods used by leaders often correlate with their cultural images. For example, if leaders see themselves as Zeus-like family figures, they seldom use democratic or participative methods and tend rather to be charismatic, directive and authoritarian. On the other hand, Athena, or team leaders, tend to be more consultative, participative and nondirective in their approach.

## METHODS REFLECT PRINCIPLES

Because of vast cultural differences, it is not possible to describe methods of leadership that are appropriate in every culture. In chapter ten we looked at a theology of leadership. Leadership methods must reflect these biblical principles.

No matter what methods leaders use, they must lead through godly example, through teaching, by focusing the vision, and by ensuring that strategies and programs contribute to the vision.[15]

In the next section we will look at practical implications for leaders in any culture.

**Table 10.1. Methodological Implications of Biblical Principles**

| Biblical Principle | Methodological Implications |
|---|---|
| 1. God made us for himself. We exist to know, love and glorify God. | Trust God, and realize that he is the ultimate leader. We are accountable to him. All our methods must promote the glory of God. |
| 2. Satan is real and wants to destroy God's plan and people. | The best methods will not guarantee results. Leaders face spiritual forces of evil. Leaders must resist temptations of the evil one. |
| 3. God created people and has a plan for the world. | Leaders must seek God's vision for their ministry. |
| 4. The Bible is God's primary communication. | Leaders must be able to teach and be held accountable to biblical truth. |
| 5. Human beings are created in the image of God and will live forever. | Leaders must never treat people as a means to an end or dehumanize those created in the image of God. |
| 6. Human beings are fallen creatures with a natural tendency for evil. | Leaders must beware of the evil tendencies in themselves and not be taken off guard by followers with selfish motives. |
| 7. God sent his son Jesus into the world to redeem us and demonstrate godly leadership. | We define "servant leader" not by our culture, but by looking at Jesus. No solution to world problems will work without the redemptive work of Jesus. |
| 8. The Holy Spirit empowers believers and gives spiritual gifts to all who know him. | Leaders must be sensitive to the leading of the Holy Spirit. Leaders must also recognize that every person has direct access to God through the Holy Spirit. Leaders must listen to others. |
| 9. God intends believers to grow into the fullness of the stature of Christ. | Methods must be evaluated by how well they help others become like Christ. Methods that hinder this process must be avoided. |
| 10. The church is a necessary means for Christians to grow in Christ. | Leaders must provide opportunities for people to interact with each other and allow the gifts of the whole body to strengthen the church. |
| 11. Jesus is coming again to judge the world. | The final evaluation of leadership effectiveness will not happen in this world. Methods of leadership must aim to produce eternal results. |
| 12. People will live forever in heaven or hell. | Evangelism is a critical means for accomplishing the task. Since people live forever and organizations come and go, the primary emphasis must be on the development of people. |

# PART IV

# GLOBAL LEADERSHIP
# IN PRACTICE

PART FOUR APPLIES INSIGHTS FROM THE BIBLE and culture to practical issues in world missions and the global church. One of the most important responsibilities of leaders is to stimulate vision. How is this done in multicultural situations? How do cultural differences impact leadership development? We will look at these and other practical issues in this section.

The down-to-earth practice of leadership grows out of a biblical understanding of the task and methods of leadership, yet is profoundly influenced by cultural differences. While the ultimate purpose, worldview, goals and methods of leadership are theological, theoretical and abstract, the practice of leadership is concrete and visible.

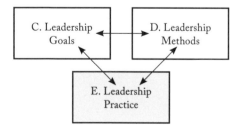

Figure IV.1

# DEVELOPING
# VISION AND STRATEGY

*To see life as it is, rather than how it should be—that is madness!*

Don Quixote, in *Man of La Mancha*, by Cervantes

*Vision without action is a daydream.*
*Action without vision is a nightmare.*

Japanese Proverb

Leaders do lots of things. They write memos, attend meetings, design plans, evaluate strategies, make decisions, answer emails, deliver speeches, organize people, delegate responsibility and talk on the phone. But what leadership really comes down to is "doing whatever it takes to fulfill the vision of the organization." The greatest danger for any organization, and especially a multicultural one, is that leaders will lose their vision while becoming proficient at strategies that take them in the wrong direction. Too often the activity replaces the outcome; the strategy replaces the vision.

During my time with SIM, I often thought about the bumper sticker my predecessor had given me: "The main thing is to keep the main thing, the main thing." My greatest fear as a multicultural leader was that we would lose our vision for the "main thing." Much of my time in leadership was given to vision and strategy seminars. In this chapter we will consider the implications for focusing vision in a multicultural context. We will look at the interconnectedness of vision, strategy and an understanding of the situation. In short, we'll look at the *practice* of leadership.

How do we actually practice leadership? As we have seen, practice grows out of assumptions about the ultimate purpose, worldview, leadership goals and methods. All are interconnected.

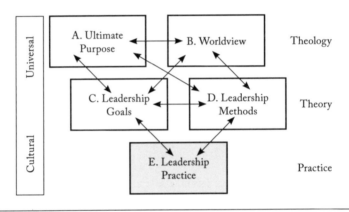

Figure 11.1. Model of crosscultural leadership

A person's theology and theory of leadership influence everything. For example, Aristotle wrote, "From the hour of birth, some are marked out for subjection, others for rule." So for Aristotle, there would be little incentive to develop leaders because he believed they were born, not made. His leadership practice would be authoritarian as he led people "marked for subjection."

One day, as four of us rode together on our hour-long commute to work, we began to discuss leadership. My colleague in the back seat threatened to write a book titled "Leaders I've Known from Hell," expounding with disgust on her wide experience of working with incompetent leaders. Soon we were outdoing each other with horror stories of bad leaders who were manipulative, arrogant and destructive. Inept leaders seldom lack technique. They are incompetent because they work from bad theory and an inadequate theology of leadership.

Why do so many bad leaders persist? What makes a good leader?
Are only a few people leaders and the rest followers? Are some people
born leaders? Why is there so little agreement about leadership traits?
Do leadership differences arise from personality or from culture? Are
leaders required to be visionaries? Do they need administrative skills?
Is there really a spiritual gift of leadership, and if so, why do so many
seemingly bungling leaders claim to have it? Can a leader be capable in
one culture and not in another? Assuming diverse cultures have different leadership values, can all of them be biblical? If a missionary team
is made up of people from six countries and all have different expectations about leadership, who needs to change? How do we know if our
leadership values are biblical or cultural? Is there a universal pattern of
good leadership?

### A NEW METAPHOR FOR LEADERSHIP

Some years ago, I wrote a controversial article for the *Evangelical Missions
Quarterly* titled "Measurable Objectives, No! Faith Goals, Yes!"[1] I was
attempting to recommend a middle way of planning that would avoid the
extremes of setting precise objectives on the one hand and simply "going
with the flow" on the other. My desire was to describe a metaphor that
had the potential of bridging both high- and low-context cultures.[2] The
objections to the article came from a low-context perspective.

When leading vision seminars, I often look at three leadership
metaphors.

### FACTORY METAPHOR

One leadership paradigm can be likened to an assembly line in a factory.[3] The factory metaphor reflects a behaviorist model and places a
high value on precision, quantitative goals, predictability, efficiency
and control. Planners set goals that can be measured readily within a
certain timeframe. The model assumes that observable behavior is the
only reality. The factory metaphor is a low-context paradigm with a
low tolerance for ambiguity.

When we aim only at what we can measure, we tend to ignore the
most important goals of spiritual formation, discipleship and holiness.

These are qualities we cannot predict or quantify without falling into legalism. Factory thinking inhibits real vision for qualitative development inside of people, in the church and in society.

## WILDFLOWER METAPHOR

In reaction to the factory model, the wildflower model emphasizes intuitive personal experience, emotions and dramatic demonstrations of God's power. While it may provide a healthy corrective to the factory metaphor, it may not be fully integrated with biblical reflection and may build blindly on insights from existentialism. The wildflower metaphor tends to be a high-context paradigm with a high tolerance for ambiguity.

This go-with-the-flow approach minimizes future planning and may even assume such planning is unspiritual. Whereas mechanistic leaders manage by objectives, existential leaders often manage by interruption.

Both the low-context factory paradigm and the high-context wildflower paradigm are inadequate. Is there a third paradigm that grows out of sound theology and is driven by vision?

## PILGRIM METAPHOR

The metaphor of pilgrimage is visionary and purposeful. Pilgrims have a goal and a sense of direction, but they realize that the path often leads through rugged mountains and foggy swamps, bringing unexpected twists and turns. Pilgrim leaders tolerate ambiguity and focus on the unfolding serendipitous opportunities that God brings into view. Because they have a sense of direction, they are better able to decide if an event is an unfolding opportunity or a sidetracking interruption. They aren't surprised by difficulty and uncertainty because they are motivated in their service by a vision of the kingdom. They depend on the help of other pilgrims as they come to know and trust the map of the Word of God.

Development is an inner process that has external (though unpredictable) indicators. The vision is not for mere behavior changes that can be predicted and controlled, but for holy lives that bring glory to God. It is a vision for the growth of the kingdom of God. Rather than seeking mere numerical growth, we pursue a vision for a glorious church, without spot or wrinkle, holy and without fault. It is a vision for what people might look like if they would enroll as lifelong students in Jesus' school of discipleship, consistently displaying the fruit of the Spirit.

The developmental pilgrim paradigm helps to bridge the strengths of both low-context and high-context cultures while minimizing the weaknesses of the two extremes. As such, it is a helpful paradigm for crosscultural leadership.

### VISIONARY PLANNING

The primary job of the leader is to make sure that the strategy fits the situation and contributes to the vision. In practice, leaders must do three things (see p. 192).

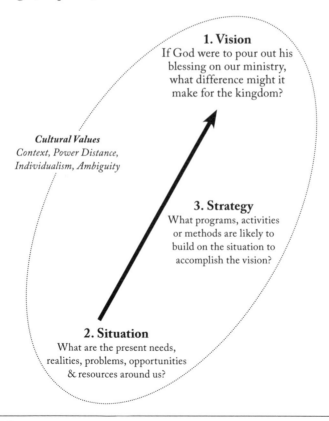

**1. Vision**
If God were to pour out his blessing on our ministry, what difference might it make for the kingdom?

*Cultural Values*
*Context, Power Distance, Individualism, Ambiguity*

**3. Strategy**
What programs, activities or methods are likely to build on the situation to accomplish the vision?

**2. Situation**
What are the present needs, realities, problems, opportunities & resources around us?

**Figure 11.2**

1. Collect and focus the *vision.*

2. Make sure that every *strategy* in the organization contributes to the vision.

3. Connect strategies to the needs and opportunities of the current *situation.*

The relationship between these components of leadership is illustrated in the previous diagram.

## VISION

*Where are we going?* Why do we exist? What is God's purpose for this organization? What is the desired outcome in the lives of people and the church that will result in eternal praise to God? Vision describes qualities in people that bring glory to God. Vision describes a picture of the kingdom of God on earth and in heaven. The outcome of vision is transformed lives, demonstrating God's love in individuals and the church.

Vision statements will vary slightly from church to church and organization to organization, but the core of each will include a picture of Christlike persons, a holy church and worship. We have seen in the previous chapter that the ultimate purpose of leadership is the glory of God in the worldwide church. The principle task is to develop people. To do this leaders must facilitate the process of discovering and focusing God's vision for a ministry.

Vision does not originate from a strong leader, nor is it derived from a mechanical process. Vision comes through the study of Scripture, prayer and dialogue. It comes through eyes of faith, glimpsing a picture of the future when God will fulfill his purposes. It originates from Holy Spirit–motivated passion to follow God's vision. Vision is from God and is a faith-picture of what could happen in the lives of people if God were to pour out his blessing.

In workshops, I often place people together in small groups to prayerfully ask the question, If God were to pour out his blessing in my ministry, what difference might it make for his kingdom? We seek vision *on our knees.*

The visionary leader has a mental picture of what God could do in the world. The ultimate purpose of an individual, a church or an organization is to be used of God to bring about his plans for time and eternity. Everything else must be subservient to the vision.

Too often, though, the actual vision drifts from the stated vision. For example a mission agency might have a vision statement that says, "Our vision is to glorify God by planting and nurturing churches in the Muslim world." But in actual fact, the real vision of the organization is simply to survive, or to double the size of the missionary force, or to raise more money. The difference between the stated and actual vision might not be intentional, but the urgent displaces the important.

All too often people become so engrossed in the strategy that they forget the intended outcome. Mark Twain made the astute observation, "for the little boy with the hammer, every problem is a nail." Strategies may unintentionally take the place of vision.

The *JESUS* film has had an amazing impact throughout the world. Suppose a missionary envisions a whole people group transformed by the gospel through the strategy of showing the film. But after a while, without noticing, the missionary may become so obsessed with how many times she can show the film, that she hurries from village to village without following up on those who respond. She may innocently rationalize that she can show the film many more times if she doesn't concern herself with nurturing new believers. It might not be intentional, but her *vision* of seeing thousands transformed by the gospel has been replaced by the strategy of merely showing the film thirty times in a month. Even though the *JESUS* film may be the most effective evangelistic tool of the century, it is a means, not an end. The method must not take the place of the vision.

For the missionary in radio ministry, the vision may be that everyone on earth have the opportunity to hear the gospel in a language they can understand. But subtly and unintentionally the ultimate vision may become fundraising. Or suppose a mission would like to provide mini reference libraries to thousands of pastors. The vision may begin with a mental picture of thousands of pastors encouraged by these study resources, preaching powerful sermons and revitalizing churches with transformational preaching. But after a few months the vision shifts to raising funds, recruiting volunteers and transporting books. When the urgency of the immediate situation supplants the original vision, people become overwhelmed and discouraged. They measure success in terms of activities, programs or numerical results instead of visionary outcomes.

Fortunately there are many examples of leaders who have rekindled vision, regained focus and moved ahead with fresh enthusiasm. I remember an incident involving a highly competent missionary in Bolivia. His original vision was to enhance the effectiveness of pastors by helping them get books that would help them with sermon preparation, counseling and their own spiritual growth. But as the project developed, he became caught up in bartering with publishers to get a good price on the greatest number of books, and he ended up with books that were of little help to pastors. The books were cheap but they didn't support the vision. As soon as he realized this subtle shift he changed course and went back to finding the best books for the pastors rather than the cheapest books. The vision again controlled the strategy, and the project was exceptionally effective.

### SITUATION

*Where are we now?* What are the present needs, problems, opportunities and resources? Strategies need to grow out of the situational realities and contribute toward accomplishing the vision. The leader needs to ask the crucial questions: Do our programs help solve real and important problems in our present situation? Do we have resources to carry out the ministry? Are opportunities unfolding around us that we can maximize? Vision challenges the leader to think big; assessing the *situation* forces leaders to be realistic.

When I travel in Latin America I collect carvings of Don Quixote and Sancho Panza, the two main characters in the Cervantes classic. Don Quixote is an unrealistic visionary, forever embarking on a quest to save the world from evil. Sancho Panza is the realist who reminds Don Quixote that he needs a horse and that the giants he sees are really windmills. Quixote has his head in the clouds, while Panza has his feet on the ground. Realists need visionaries, and visionaries need realists who understand the current needs, opportunities and resources of the situation.

I remember receiving a phone call from a visionary missionary in Africa. He waxed eloquent about his many ideas, and proceeded to tell me all the things I, as the mission director needed to do about his vision. I asked, "Have you been able to make progress on any of your ideas?" He remonstrated, "I am a visionary, not someone who gets bogged down with programs." I replied that he needed to partner with someone who could help him implement his vision. The last thing I needed was more visionaries who weren't able to get anything done. The Quixotes need the Panzas; the idealists need the realists; and the visionaries need people who are well aware of the needs and limitations of the present situation.

Another reason to be attuned to the situation is that it is always changing. And when the situation changes, programs also need to change. For example, if people in Africa begin to listen to FM radio rather than shortwave, then radio stations must figure out a way to shift to FM broadcasting. The situation has changed, so strategy must change. Activities often take on a life of their own no matter how irrelevant they are to meeting the needs of the situation.

During my years in SIM, I often met with the senior leadership to spend a whole day doing a SWOT analysis. SWOT stands for *strengths, weaknesses, opportunities* and *threats*. For example, we needed to make a decision about whether we should investigate a merger with another large mission. We spent half the morning discussing the *strengths* of such a merger, and then moved to a long list of *weaknesses* in the plan. In the afternoon we looked ahead to the future *opportunities* a merger might bring, but balanced this with potential *threats* of joining the two missions.

An analysis of the situation needs clear thinking with open debate. Peter Drucker writes, "The first rule in decision-making is that one does not make a decision unless there is disagreement."[4] He goes on to describe a meeting where everyone was in agreement on a certain decision. The chair of the meeting then postponed the agenda item until the next meeting so as to have time to develop disagreement.

When I chair a meeting, I have found this approach to be helpful. I intentionally ask for someone to speak to the opposing view. Brutal honesty is needed in an analysis of the situation. Questions to ask include the following:

- Of the hundreds of opportunities in our present situation, which are most related to our vision?

- What are the felt and real needs of the people to whom we minister?

- What unfolding opportunities are we not aware of?

- What resources do we have or lack to initiate a new program?

- Which programs are no longer meeting the needs of the present situation?

## STRATEGY

*How do we get there?* Strategy describes steps toward accomplishing the vision. What practical programs or activities are likely to be used of God to fulfill the vision? Without strategy, vision is only a dream. I just finished reading a weekly email asking prayer for strategies such as a Marriage Encounter Seminar in Uruguay, radio programs in Bolivia and Liberia, flood relief projects in Bangladesh, medical caravans in Ecuador, a program in Benin for mothers, and a health center in Sudan. It is not enough for leaders to be visionaries. Leaders are called to take bold, creative action to fulfill the vision.

Strategy grows out of vision and an understanding of the situation. Strategies are like stepping stones across the river, and the vision is represented by the far shore. By faith, we see short-term goals that can be used of God to accomplish the vision.

It is crucial for faith strategies to grow out of vision. For example, a short-term missions team may desire to glorify God by helping to construct an orphanage, but in the urgency to complete a building they offend local people, making them feel inadequate. The visiting team may return home with a sense of superiority and disdain for the people in the needy community. The strategy of completing a building displaced the ultimate vision of glorifying God through helping people, and has in fact done harm. The completion of the building subtly replaced the glory of God.

Without vision, leaders lack focus and people tend to do whatever seems right in their own eyes. Great confusion, competition and tension results when missionaries work on individualistic strategies without an overarching vision. Yet dozens of excellent examples illustrate strategies that are nurtured by vision.

> Tim and Sarah have spent forty years in Asia building trusting relationships with Christians. Now they are being invited to train pastors and teachers in six provinces of China. Their vision is to train leaders in the church and society to advance the Kingdom of God in China. To implement their vision, they have initiated annual retreats with 25 key leaders. From these conferences, a new missionary sending agency has emerged. This Chinese-led mission organization is presently surveying, planning and recruiting missionaries to penetrate less-reached people groups in China. Another strategy driven by their vision is a Christian bookstore which will provide infrastructure for leadership training. The bookstore includes a "Books for Pastors" program. By emphasizing leadership development, Tim and Sarah's ministry is impacting people at every stage of the faith journey—from evangelism to a mature church.[5]

It seems that the natural tendency is for short-term strategies to migrate into the place of vision. Strategies are immediate, concrete and practical, while vision is abstract. It is easy to neglect or forget the original compelling vision. I once heard an African proverb that says, "When you are up to your knees in crocodiles, it is easy to forget the original vision of draining the swamp."

Suppose a missions pastor envisions a church that has such great love for God and passion for worship that the people will eagerly reach out to their multiethnic neighborhood to tell others about their wonderful Savior. In order to accomplish the vision, he develops strategies of exposing the congregation to the neighborhood and training them in crosscultural evangelism. He may begin by taking small groups around the city on culture trips, setting up training sessions and bringing in people of other cultures from the neighborhood to tell about their lives. Strategies grow out of vision.

## CULTURAL VALUES

Vision planning always takes place within the larger cultural context. High- and low-context leaders will use the model differently. How does one know which paradigm is which? Most of the time we must deduce the cultural values about leadership through observation. An anthropologist conducting an ethnographic study of a rural church in Asia would need to observe the practice of leadership and ask many questions to begin to understand the big cultural picture. Who are the formal leaders, and which people are behind-the-scenes influencers? How does one become a leader? What does the leader wear, and does he or she wear clothing different from nonleaders? Does the leader sit in a different kind of chair in a different place? How do people greet the leader? How does the leader spend his or her day? What cultural values is the leader trying to preserve? What are the intended outcomes of leadership? Can we discover what people think of the spirit world? What is the vision for the community?

Read the following description by Tabitha Plueddemann as she visited the Emir of Kano, Nigeria, where her parents were missionaries. Note the cultural values about leadership that can be inferred from this description.

> My mother, sister and I pried off our slippers and passed barefoot under the massive mahogany door frame into the cool shadows of the throne room. At the far end, Emir Alhaji Ado Bayero of Kano sat dignified and cross-legged on a raised platform. Draped in mounds of ceremonial regalia, he looked like a mountain capped off by a large white turban with two rabbit-like ears projecting from the top. Gaudy lights were strung back and forth across the mud wall above his head.
>
> We dropped to our knees and bowed till our foreheads brushed the dirt floor and acquired the compulsory spot of dust. Then, having been advised never to turn our backs on the Emir, we stood and stepped backwards until we blinked uncomfortably in the sunshine.[6]

## LEADERSHIP AND CULTURE

We've seen that different cultures have distinctive ways of thinking about vision, strategy and the situation. Low-context leaders prefer a precise vision, while high-context leaders are comfortable with ambiguity and have a general idea of what they would like to accomplish. Leaders with a low tolerance for ambiguity conduct a detailed audit of their situation including resources and a professional needs analysis. Leaders with a high tolerance for ambiguity seem to intuitively understand the situation and don't feel they need a lot of data. They prefer a short-term plan assuming a continually changing situation.

Leaders with different cultural values use the same model, but they use it in a very different way.

Being aware of cultural differences is a valuable first step for the leader working between two cultures. The second step is to seek to integrate the strengths of high- and low-context values. The pilgrim leader challenges high-context people to work toward a more definite "faith picture" of results, and encourages the low-context leader to be more open to unexpected outcomes. He or she will seek to sharpen the strategic focus of high-context leaders, while helping low-context leaders to be more open to unfolding opportunities resulting from serendipitous changes. The pilgrim leader will help low-context team members to appreciate insights from an instinctive analysis of the situation, and help high-context team members to appreciate insights from a more objective analysis of the situation.

As leaders in the worldwide body of Christ interact more and more with each other, greater need for cooperative visionary planning develops. The rich harmony of multicultural teams is worth the cultural stretching we are called to do!

# DEVELOPING GLOBAL LEADERS

*If God has given you leadership ability, take the responsibility seriously.*

Romans 12:8 nlt

*From the hour of birth, some are marked out for
subjection and others to rule.*

Aristotle

If Aristotle is correct, leadership development is a waste of time. He says leaders are born, not made, so why bother with trying to develop leaders? Scripture teaches that leadership is a gift of God. If that is so, do human beings need to be concerned with developing leaders? After all, the words "leadership development" are not found in the Bible. Jesus spent three years on earth developing disciples, or followers—not leaders. In many cultures, leadership is inherited or ascribed by age and is unrelated to level of education or individual qualifications.

## LEADERSHIP DEVELOPMENT AND FORMAL EDUCATION

During my time as director of theological education for the Evangelical Churches of West Africa (ECWA) I met with a number of frustrated

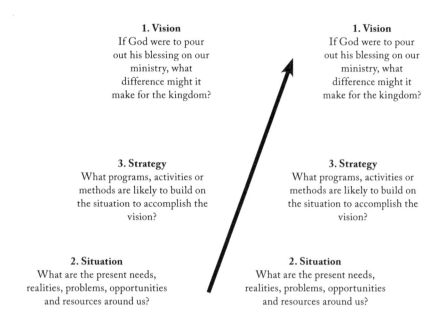

**1. Vision**
If God were to pour out his blessing on our ministry, what difference might it make for the kingdom?

**1. Vision**
If God were to pour out his blessing on our ministry, what difference might it make for the kingdom?

**3. Strategy**
What programs, activities or methods are likely to build on the situation to accomplish the vision?

**3. Strategy**
What programs, activities or methods are likely to build on the situation to accomplish the vision?

**2. Situation**
What are the present needs, realities, problems, opportunities and resources around us?

**2. Situation**
What are the present needs, realities, problems, opportunities and resources around us?

**High-Context Culture**          **Low-Context Culture**

| Vision | is intuitive with a general sense of direction. | Vision | is precise with predictable and quantifiable objectives. |
|---|---|---|---|
| Strategy | often arises from unexpected opportunities and spontaneously changes when the situation changes. | Strategy | is planned far in advance and is tightly evaluated in light of measurable objectives. |
| Situation | comes from an instinctive reading of the environment. | Situation | is analytically and logically analyzed. |

**Figure 11.3**

graduates of Nigerian Bible colleges and seminaries. They had just sacrificed years of their lives and significant amounts of money to become pastoral leaders of churches, but they found that the uneducated older pastors didn't want to relinquish their authority to young people. Now they were unemployed. When I discussed the matter with the older pastors, they were astounded that these "young boys," not half their age, had the audacity to try and take over their leadership positions. For them, age, experience and reputation—not education —were the requirements for church leadership. They quoted 1 Timothy 3, pointing out that the qualifications for a church leader include reputation, experience and family life. Education is never mentioned.

Robert Banks has written on theological education and observes that most theological schools claim their curriculum is designed to produce servant leaders.[1] He cites research showing that the findings about developing leaders are "not encouraging."[2] Ted Ward questions the relationship between formal education and leadership: "Leadership education for the church is dominated by an intellectual meritocracy. . . . Intellectual meritocracy is a kind of aristocracy; it should be challenged within the church because it falls short of the standards for community that are described biblically as the community of Christ."[3] Theological education has the potential of fostering an arrogance of credentials, which is counterproductive in developing servant leaders. I suggest that the problem is not so much that seminaries are doing a bad job, but that even the best seminary education plays only a secondary role in developing leaders. The gifting of the Spirit and leadership experience are the primary means for developing leaders.

Why do theological schools claim to be developing leaders if formal education is not a necessary criteria for leadership and may even hinder the process? Why do organizations send people to leadership courses when there is no evidence that education turns bad leaders into good leaders? Ted Ward has given an interesting answer: "The educational institution should not be in the business of creating preachers, ministers, and church leadership people, but of equipping leadership people. To serve the church, education should be broadly committed to equipping the saints in the roles, tasks and ministries to which they are called."[4]

Schooling, short courses, seminars, and books on leadership are often valuable tools for informing and encouraging leaders, but only because these have the potential of enhancing the leadership gifts God has already given. Schools, books and seminars don't produce good leaders, but they can provide valuable insights and "fan into flame" the leadership gifts God has already given.

## LEADERSHIP DEVELOPMENT AND CULTURE

Cultural differences in leadership expectations have often caught me off guard. Most of us who grew up in the United Sates have assumed that anyone can learn to be a leader and everyone desires personal advancement. Michael Hoppe describes assumptions about North American leadership:[5]

- Leadership development is the development of individuals.

- Leadership development is personal development.

- Almost everybody can develop leadership capacities.

- Leadership can be learned.

- Personal advancement is desirable.

- Being open to change is good.

- Practical experience is good.

- Improvement and progress are normal.

- Taking action is essential.

- Objective feedback is good.

Hoppe writes, "U.S. leadership development courses tend to focus on the individual as leader rather than conceptualizing leadership as a function of the group or organization as a whole."[6]

Because of my background I assumed that anyone who worked hard enough could be upwardly mobile. When we arrived in Nigeria I was surprised to find thoroughly different cultural assumptions about leadership development. Historically the path for status mobility in the Hausa culture was to be a loyal client of a patron in a higher position. When the patron received a promotion he would bring his loyal followers along with him. Leadership development could actually be hindered by individual initiative. The client who was the most loyal and helpful to his patron would be the one most likely to receive a political appointment.[7] On the other hand, the Igbo of southeastern Nigeria were traditionally a "classless society, with rule by consensus, great emphasis on individual achievement, and traditionally no great differences in economic status."[8] Between these two cultures are the Yoruba of south-western Nigeria. Traditionally, the king was selected from one of the royal lineage families, based on family ties and personal character. The final selection was made by a council of the senior chiefs who consulted an oracle.[9]

In a single African country we find three substantially different cultural assumptions about leadership development. Leadership development in these three cultures took place though loyalty to a patron (Hausa), individual effort (Igbo) and royal lineage (Yoruba). Few of the American assumptions about leadership would be culturally appropriate in traditional Nigeria. It would be absurd to expect that a foreign "expert" could teach a leadership course in Nigeria without an understanding of the traditional cultural assumptions about how leaders are developed.

The way cultures evaluate leadership potential depends on values. So in Hausa societies, potential candidates are loyal and devoted to a patron. Among the Igbo, potential leaders work hard and take individual initiative. Yoruba king-makers look for family lineage in seeking out potential leaders.

Even though we find great differences in cultural assumptions for developing leaders, I'm convinced that there are models that will be useful in any culture. I believe this because of the universal aspects of human nature and because there are biblical principles that are relevant in the worldwide body of Christ.

### PROBLEMS EXPAND HORIZONS

One of the primary tasks of leadership development is to help people to think bigger, to broaden their horizons, and to enlarge their perspectives. I am convinced that the most effective leaders are those who have the broadest perspectives.

Why is it that some of the most experienced leaders are the least effective in multicultural situations? If people think they already know everything they need to know about leadership, they stop growing. Leaders with one year of experience repeated twenty times have not learned from experience. *The primary stimulus for human development is problems—life challenges and situations that don't make sense.* Disequilibration is the motor that drives leadership development. The teaching of James is relevant here. "Consider it pure joy, my brothers and sisters, whenever you face trials of many kinds, because you know that the testing of your faith produces perseverance . . . that you may be mature and complete, not lacking anything" (Jas 1:2-4).

Jean Piaget pioneered research on how children learn to make sense out of the world. "People tend to grow and develop as they struggle with problems in the social setting. Interestingly, people tend to make the most progress in learning when things don't make sense!"[10]

My world exploded when I went to college. Until then I thought I had a pretty good grasp on the world and the meaning of life. I lived in a world of certainties where my family and church friends had similar ideas about theology, politics, sports and economics. On the first day of classes I discovered that Gabe, my freshman roommate, was a Democrat—and I wasn't sure if Democrats were going to heaven. One morning I woke up to see my roommate on his knees, reading his Bible and praying. Was it possible that my dad was wrong about Democrats? How could my dad be wrong about anything? It didn't bother me too much that my non-Michigan classmates didn't like the Detroit Pistons, Tigers or Lions, but if my political certainties were shattered, what might happen to my theology?

My philosophy professor, Dr. Hackett, stymied me with the question, "If a tree falls in the forest and no one hears it, does it make a sound?" I never thought about that before or about many other questions that he posed. Was the world really created in 4004 B.C. like my study Bible taught? Did Moses use documents from other sources in writing the Pentateuch? Was the Vietnam conflict a just war? Was Horace Bushnell a liberal heretic when he wrote that "a child is to grow up a Christian and never know himself as being otherwise"?[11]

We develop when our world is shaken, when our comfort zone of certainty is challenged. My immature individualism was upset as family and friends challenged me to wrestle with conflicting ideas. My horizons radically broadened when the ripples of my comfortable hometown pond were widened by college friends and professors.

## PERSPECTIVE AND LEADERSHIP DEVELOPMENT

How can egocentric and family-centric leaders move toward seeing the world from an ever-broadening perspective? Most studies show that perspective transformation is not learned through courses on theories of leadership or elaborate management techniques. Perspective transformation develops by reflecting on disequilibrating experiences and through disorienting dilemmas.[12] In other words, leaders don't develop if they don't face challenging situations.

God broadened Abraham's perspective by the disorienting experience of leaving the comfort zone of his country, people and father's household and moving from Ur to Canaan—a journey of over a thousand miles. God broadened Abraham's worldview and stretched his faith through waiting and testing. Later God widened his vision by promising him a land with precise boundaries and within a specific timeframe. The Lord developed Abraham as a leader by broadening him from a family-centric nomad to become the father of many nations and the channel of blessing for all the peoples of the earth. He did this by fostering experiences that would test his faith.

Moses was the most powerful leader in all of Israel. The Lord took the son of lowly slaves and widened his horizon by placing him in Pharaoh's household. He enlarged his perspective even more by apprenticing him to a shepherd on the back side of the desert and then stretching his weak faith through the burning bush and giving him practice in performing miracles. God's curriculum for Moses' leadership development did not take place in a classroom but through challenging experiences that shifted his worldview. He changed from being an egocentric young man in Pharaoh's court to seeing the world from God's perspective.

Throughout history the most powerful leaders, for good or for evil, have been those with the broadest perspective. The exploits of Genghis Khan demonstrate the ability of a leader to move beyond family-centered collectivism to become the powerful leader of a unified Mongol army and ruler of a vast empire.

In twenty-five years, the Mongol army subjugated more lands and people than the Romans had conquered in four hundred years. Genghis

Khan, together with his sons and grandsons, conquered the most densely populated civilizations of the thirteenth century. Whether measured by the total number of people defeated, the sum of the countries annexed, or by the total area occupied, Genghis Khan conquered more than twice as much as any man in history.[13]

To accomplish this, Genghis Khan had to overcome kinship and clan loyalties that fragmented the Mongol people. His new organization abolished clans and tribes by creating a *multination-centered* collectivism where everyone—no matter their status at birth or family ties—would be part of a united people.[14] Instead of making conquered people slaves, he accepted the entire tribe or nation into his empire as family members, creating a universal citizenship.[15] "At the zenith, the empire covered between 11 and 12 million contiguous square miles, an area about the size of the African continent and considerably larger than North America, including the United States, Canada, Mexico, Central America and the islands of the Caribbean combined."[16] Genghis Khan developed from being part of a low-caste and rejected family to become one of the most outstanding leaders in all of history. While his exploits are a mix of good and evil, his story demonstrates the principle that the most influential leaders have the widest horizons.

One of the primary tasks of leadership development is fostering the growth of wider perspectives in potential leaders. The levels of leadership perspective might be summarized as follows:

1. *The egocentric individualistic leader* looks out for his or her own interests.

2. *The family-centric collectivistic leader* promotes the good of the extended family but will not trust those outside the family.

3. *The ethno-centric collectivistic leader* promotes the good of his or her church, denomination, organization or country, but assumes that the rest of the world can and should follow a similar model of success.

4. *The global-centric leader* will look out for the good of the individual, family, clan and nation, within the context of the bigger picture. The godly world-centric leader will see fleeting glimpses of the world from God's perspective and approach a theo-centric perspective. The

theo-centric leader will care for individuals and seek the good of his or her organization, but not at the expense of hurting other groups. Such leaders orient their horizons toward universal principles and often blur the distinction between individualism and collectivism.

By God's grace leaders can develop through these levels of leadership perspective. Egocentric individualist leaders can learn to care selflessly for the needs of a group. Family-centric leaders can be nurtured to understand the broader perspective of the larger group or organization. Ethnocentric collectivists have the potential of maturing toward a global perspective of the worldwide body of Christ. The Lord allows leaders to experience disequilibrating situations that have the potential of transforming their perspectives.

## A MODEL OF LEADERSHIP DEVELOPMENT

In spite of significant differences, every culture must find ways to develop leaders. These four steps are effective across cultures:[17]

1. Seek out people with high leadership potential.

2. Assess their current strengths and weaknesses.

3. Challenge them with tasks that are slightly beyond their comfort zone.

4. Support them in the tasks.

First, *seek out people with high leadership potential*. Each year the senior leadership team of our mission would go on a four-day retreat. One of the main items on the agenda was to confidentially identify high-potential women and men to be selected for broader leadership positions. We collected names of high-potential people from all the country directors and added our own reflections. Usually several potential leaders showed up on a number of lists. Selecting high-potential leaders was a communal activity.

Potential leaders prove themselves through smaller leadership tasks. They are possibility thinkers who are able to work with others to accomplish a crucial task. Faithful servants who do well in handling smaller tasks show they are ready for more responsibility (Mt 25:21).

Second, *assess their current strengths and weaknesses.* Our senior team prayerfully discussed each person who was recommended. We talked about their skills and experiences as well as areas of inexperience and weakness. We made a point to find ways to get to know them better. We found it was important to assess potential leaders before they were given additional responsibilities. We also committed to praying regularly for the high-potential leaders we had identified.

Third, find ways to *challenge potential leaders with tasks that are slightly beyond their comfort zone.* The learning experience needs to be slightly disequilibrating. If the job is too easy, leaders won't learn and grow. If it is too hard, they might become discouraged and quit. We would often look for assignments that would take developing leaders to a different part of the world. Once we asked talented youth workers from Bolivia to lead a workshop in Nigeria. At first the couple was intimidated, thinking they couldn't possibly be effective on another continent. They succeeded beyond anything they could imagine. The experience broadened their horizons and built their confidence.

Fourth, *support them in the tasks.* We did everything we could to help men and women succeed in the challenging tasks we gave them. I remember working hard with a woman who was asked to take on a new leadership role. She was feeling overwhelmed and quite unsure of her ability to do the job. I talked about strengths that the senior leadership team saw in her. I reminded her of past successful leadership experiences. I suggested books that might help her. I put her in touch with another expert in the country where she would serve. My wife and I visited her in her new role. She did an excellent job.

I'll admit that the model didn't work all the time. One high-potential leader was given a task beyond him and in spite of a good deal of support, he didn't do well. The experience damaged his self-confidence for years. What did we do wrong? Did we miss out in our assessment of this person? Did we give him a task that was too challenging too soon? Was there more we could have done to support him? The failure continues to plague me. Yet on the whole, this model has served well in many cultural settings.

As I look back on my life, some of the most fulfilling moments come from turning over my leadership role to a person from another culture. I praise the Lord for these leaders who continued to do a better job than I ever could.

EPILOGUE

# LEADERSHIP IN THE
# GLOBAL CHURCH

*Our natural tendency is to watch the world from behind the windows*
*of [our] cultural home and to act as if people from other countries,*
*ethnicities, or categories have something special about them, . . .*
*but [our] home is normal. Awareness means the discovery*
*that there is no normal position in cultural matters.*

GEERT HOFSTEDE, FOREWORD TO *LEADERSHIP IN*
*A DIVERSE AND MULTICULTURAL ENVIRONMENT*

SUPPOSE A DOZEN BLIND PEOPLE ARE LOCKED in a large room. No one
can talk. After bumping around for a few days, they begin to develop
signals that prevent them from colliding with each other. By stamping
their feet as they walk, they communicate location and direction. Even-

tually they build a strong sense of community. After a couple of months another dozen blind people enter the room. These newcomers had previously constructed a different system of signals to promote cooperation. Instead of stamping their feet, they clap their hands as they walk. Naturally the new folks begin to stumble into the original residents, causing harsh criticism on both sides. Each group thinks the other uncultured. The clappers accuse the stompers of being rude, and the stompers assume the clappers are overly emotional. Eventually the two cultures realize their blindness and work out a new system of collaboration.

The good news is that leaders from around the world are partnering in ministry. We are all recognizing our blindness and are learning to be sensitive to the values of others. The continuing frustration often comes from the clash of leadership expectations between cultural values. Even though global cooperation will always be pestered by misunderstanding in this fallen world, a growing understanding, appreciation and harmony is possible and necessary.

Like those in the parable, we need to recognize:

1. We are often blind to the influence of our own cultural values. We need to analyze and better understand our hidden assumptions.

2. The groups we partner with may also be blind to their leadership values. Any particular system, while different, might not be better or worse than our own.

3. We can harmonize divergent cultural systems and cooperate in global ministries.

If you are a leader from an individualistic culture working with collectivistic partners:

• Recognize that there are strengths in collectivistic leadership.

• Praise the group (rather than individuals) for successes, and don't be surprised if your group is praised for your individual good work.

• Design plans in groups rather than between two people.

• Evaluate ministry by groups rather than by individual performance appraisals.

- Be patient when working toward decisions with deliberative, collectivistic cultures.

- Recognize that collectivistic societies view teams as close-knit families with each person an integral part of the whole.

If you are a leader from a collectivistic culture working with individualistic partners:

- Recognize that there are strengths in individualistic leadership.

- Don't be embarrassed when you as an individual are praised, and feel free to commend others for their individual successes.

- When designing joint plans, don't be surprised to be working with an individual rather than a group.

- Don't be offended by individual appraisal interviews.

- Be patient when working toward decisions with fast-moving individualistic partners.

- Recognize that individualistic societies view teams as temporary communities that exist to solve a problem. Teams function more like corporations than as families.

## A CULTURE OF GRACE

Multicultural mission agencies and other global organizations will thrive in settings where all are working hard to understand one another, where it's safe to change and adapt, and where relationships lead to trust. Here are some practical recommendations that came out of recent SIM workshops on multicultural team training:

- Include issues of cultural differences at every level of leadership orientation.

- Don't assume that the language of the majority of the team will be the team language. Power tends to flow, subtly or overtly, to those who are able to debate in their mother tongue.

- Be aware that one team member might be from a nation or group that in the past humiliated and tortured the ancestors of another team member.

- As far as biblically valid, let the host culture lead in forming the values and habits of team life.

- Play together.

- Share food, customs and holiday traditions of members' homelands.

- Encourage compromise in cultural preferences; discourage (even confront) extremes.

- Pray continually that team members will be "like-minded, having the same love, being one in spirit and purpose" (Phil 2:2 NIV).[1]

The worldwide body of Christ will move beyond conflict and compromise toward beautiful harmony as we understand the weaknesses of our own culture and seek out the strengths of the other. The more we move toward becoming like Christ, the further we move away from the limitations of both high-context and low-context cultures while incorporating the strengths of both. The closer we come to being transformed into the image of Christ the more fully we develop as individuals, while also becoming more deeply embedded in the richness of the global family of God.

The business world is zealous about learning to function in a globalizing society. "The global leader is open and flexible in approaching others, can cope with situations and people disparate from his or her background, and is willing to reexamine and alter personal attitudes and perceptions."[2] How much more should the church be passionate about working together as the worldwide body of Christ in a culture of grace.

Now is the time for a loving revolution in our understanding and practice of leadership. If leaders from the north and south, east and west continue with culturally blind leadership assumptions, the body of Christ will remain fragmented and disjointed. The task of world missions will be in a state of confusion and mistrust.

I have a dream of high- and low-context leaders from around the world accepting differences and working together with a sense of humor, mutual trust and delight. I picture loving cooperation between those with a high and low tolerance for ambiguity, learning to work joyfully together in ministry to unreached people groups. I envision missionaries from individualistic and collectivistic cultures learning from each other in high performance teams. In my mind's eye, I see professors from high- and low-power-distance countries, as best friends, teaching together in seminaries and Bible schools around the world.

Love must be the defining mark of leadership in the worldwide church. It is not enough to have knowledge of cultural differences or to be experts in the mysteries of leadership techniques. In the words of 1 Corinthians 13, such leaders merely produce a resounding gong and a clanging cymbal. In spite of the clash of leadership values, love is patient, love is kind, it does not boast, is not proud, does not dishonor others and is not self-seeking. It always trusts, always hopes and always perseveres (1 Cor 13:4-7). Love "binds us together in perfect harmony" (Col 3:14 ESV).

My colleague Howard Brant writes:

> There is a unique contribution every nation has to make in global missions. When one part is missing, it is as if part of a great orchestra is silent. In the divine symphony, the West has played a leading part for several hundred years. Others have had lesser parts or been silent all together. But now in these days, the Divine Conductor is turning to all parts of his orchestra and bringing it all into one grand finale. As the last score is being played, every part of the orchestra is required to play passionately, at maximum strength. What a huge disappointment if—in the last crescendo—individuals or a section of players are silent or drop out! This is the time for the whole church to be passionately involved in global missions.[3]

The choir is warming up as people from every nation, language and people gather to sing hallelujah before the throne of God. Now is the time for leaders in the global household of God to join together as never before. Let the grand symphony begin.

# NOTES

## Introduction

[1]Geert Hofstede, foreword to *Leadership in a Diverse and Multicultural Environment,* by Mary L. Connerly and Paul B. Pedersen (Thousand Oaks, Calif.: Sage Publications, 2005), p. ix.

[2]See the discussion of mission terms in A. Scott Moreau, Gary R. Corwin and Gary B. McGee, eds., *Introducing World Missions* (Grand Rapids: Baker, 2004), p. 17.

[3]For insights on the missionary outreach of religious orders, see the chapter by Mark Noll, "Catholic Reform and the Worldwide Outreach: The Founding of the Jesuits (1540)," in *Turning Points: Decisive Moments in the History of Christianity* (Grand Rapids: Baker, 1997), pp. 197-220.

[4]See the discussion by Eckhard J. Schnabel, *Paul the Missionary: Realities, Strategies and Methods* (Downers Grove, Ill.: InterVarsity Press, 2008), pp. 22-27.

[5]The terms "missional" and "mission of God" *(missio Dei)* must include "missions" and "missionary." *Missional* often is referred to as all the activities of a local church, the mission of God or all God's activities in the world. I suggest that a local church is not truly missional unless it is, among other things, sending missionaries. Look again at the comments by Eckhard Schnabel, *Paul the Missionary,* pp. 21, 22.

[6]See James E. Plueddemann, "Theological Implications of Globalizing Missions," in *Globalizing Theology,* ed. Craig Ott and Harold A. Netland (Grand Rapids: Baker, 2006), pp. 259-66.

[7]Amanda Ruggeri, "America's Best Leaders: How They Were Picked," *U.S. News & World Report,* December 8, 2008, p. 55.

[8]Ibid.

## Chapter 1: Leadership for a New Day in World Missions

[1]Geert Hofstede and Gert Jan Hofstede, *Cultures and Organizations: Software of the Mind,* 2nd ed. (New York: McGraw-Hill, 2005), pp. 116-22.

[2]Jim Collins, *Good to Great and the Social Sector* (Bolder, Colo.: privately printed, 2005), pp. 9-13.

[3]Thomas L. Friedman, *The World Is Flat* (New York: Farrar, Straus & Giroux, 2005), pp. 416-19.

[4]For a summary of these trends see James E. Plueddemann, "Theological Implications of Globalizing Missions," in *Globalizing Theology,* ed. Craig Ott and Harold A. Netland (Grand Rapids: Baker, 2006), pp. 259-66.

[5]We served with SIM for twenty-four years. SIM was formerly known as Sudan Interior Mission and is now called Serving In Mission.

## Chapter 3: Why Crosscultural Leadership?

[1]Charlie Davis, "Making Disciples Before They Believe," *Horizons* 3, no. 2 (2008): 80-81.

[2]Taken from a prayer letter written by Ken and Marilyn Foster on November 11, 2007. Used with permission.

[3]"Spiritual Journey of a Quechua Leader," SIM website (October 19, 2006) <www .sim.org>.

[4]Dietrich Bonhoeffer, *The Cost of Discipleship* (New York: Macmillan, 1963), p. 53.

[5]"Wodaabe Believers Declare Their Faith," under "Passing It On and On and On," SIM website (March 1, 2006) <www.sim.org/index.php/content/passing-it-on-and-on-and-on>.

[6]Eckhard J. Schnabel, *Early Christian Mission*, vol. 2: *Paul and the Early Church* (Downers Grove, Ill.: InterVarsity Press, 2004), p. 1425.

[7]Ibid., p. 1428.

[8]Paul Hiebert, *Anthropological Insights for Missionaries* (Grand Rapids: Baker, 1985), pp. 199-224.

[9]Tokunboh Adeyemo, ed., *Africa Bible Commentary: A One-Volume Commentary Written by 70 African Scholars* (Grand Rapids: Zondervan, 2006).

[10]One of the pioneer African evangelical theologians was Byang H. Kato. His books *African Cultural Revolution and the Christian Faith* (Jos, Nigeria: Challenge, 1976); and *Biblical Christianity in Africa* (Achimota, Ghana: African Christian Press, 1985) challenged his readers to avoid syncretism by being Christian Africans, living under the authority of Scripture.

[11]See Tite Tiénou, *The Theological Task of the Church in Africa*, 2nd ed. (Achimota, Ghana: African Christian Press, 1990).

[12]Tabitha Plueddemann, "A Stud in My Nose: God's Grace in the Latino Mission Movement," *Serving in Mission Together* 119, Fall 2007, pp. 4-7.

## Chapter 4: Leadership, Cultural Values and the Bible

[1]A quotation attributed to Lord Acton (1834-1902) in a letter to Bishop Mandell Creighton in 1887 <http://www.phrases.org.uk/meanings/288200.html>.

[2]This is what philosophers call the "naturalistic fallacy." The idea that biblical *descriptions* are leadership *prescriptions* is a dangerous concept. The naturalistic fallacy is a common problem in books on leadership. Too often, authors begin with a culturally biased principle of leadership and then find Bible verses to support their bias.

[3]For a similar description of the three levels, see Fons Trompenaars and Charles Hampden-Turner, *Riding the Waves of Culture: Understanding Cultural Diversity in Business*, 2nd ed. (London: Nicholas Brealey, 1997), p. 22. Their three levels are (1) basic assumptions, (2) norms and values, and (3) artifacts and products. I am adapting my model on that of William K. Frankena, *Philosophy of Education* (New York: Macmillan, 1965), p. 9. I am defining worldview as Frankena's box A and B—the statement of basic ends and premises about human nature, life and the world. The level of values is Frankena's box C and D, or the list of excellences and knowledge about how to produce excellences. The outer level of practices is similar to Fran-

kena's concrete conclusions.

[4]For an excellent discussion of worldview see chapter 18 of Paul G. Hiebert, *Cultural Anthropology* (Grand Rapids: Baker, 1983); and Paul G. Hiebert, *Transforming Worldviews: An Anthropological Understanding of How People Change* (Grand Rapids: Baker Academic, 2008). Chapter 1 gives an overview of the history and concept of worldview.

[5]For a discussion of the four ancient temperaments see the Wikipedia article, "Four Temperaments" <http://en.wikipedia.org/wiki/Four_Temperaments>.

[6]John W. Berry, Ype H. Portinga, Marshall H. Segall and Pierre R. Dassen, *Crosscultural Psychology: Research and Applications*, 2nd ed. (New York: Cambridge University Press, 2002), p. 86.

[7]Samuel P. Huntington, *The Clash of Civilizations and the Remaking of World Order* (New York: Simon & Schuster, 1996), p. 21. While this book is controversial because it cites religion and culture rather than political ideology as a major divisive force, the book has gained credibility since the attacks of September 11, 2001.

[8]Thomas L. Friedman, *The Lexus and the Olive Tree: Understanding Globalization* (New York: Farrar, Straus & Giroux, 1999), pp. 27-28.

[9]Edward T. Hall, *Beyond Culture* (Garden City, N.Y.: Anchor Press, 1976), pp. 16-17.

## Chapter 5: Leadership and Context

[1]Edward T. Hall, *Beyond Culture* (Garden City, N.Y.: Anchor Press, 1976), p. 15.

[2]Ibid., p. 12.

[3]Ibid., p. 91.

[4]There may also be a connection between cognitive style and preferences for event orientation or idea orientation, as described in Herman Witkin and John Berry, "Psychological Differentiation in Crosscultural Perspective," *Journal of Crosscultural Psychology* 6 (1975): 4-87. Field-independent cultures are likely to function from the perspective of an idea-orientation, and those from field-dependent cultures are more likely to be event-oriented.

[5]High and low context may be related to Plato's concept of the *noumena* (the thought or idea) and *phenomena* (the perception). High-context cultures might be called phenomena-oriented, while low-context cultures would be noumena-oriented.

[6]Mary L. Connerly and Paul B. Pedersen, *Leadership in a Diverse and Multicultural Environment* (Thousand Oaks, Calif.: Sage, 2005), p. 47.

[7]An interview with Oscar Muriu, "The African Church Planter," *Christianity Today*, posted online May 1, 2007 <http://www.christianvisionproject.com/2007/05/the_african_planter.html>. Used by permission.

[8]Hall, *Beyond Culture*, pp. 17-24.

[9]One wonders if technology is changing the cultural value of time. Could it be that the younger multitasking generation in North America is becoming more polychronic?

[10]Hall, *Beyond Culture*, p. 17.

[11]Johann Buis, quoted in Chris Blumhofer, "Music of the Spheres," *Wheaton* (Alumni magazine) 11, no. 1 (Winter 2008): 62.

## Chapter 6: Leadership and Power

[1]Bernard M. Bass and Ruth Bass, *The Bass Handbook of Leadership: Theory, Research,*

*and Managerial Applications*, 4th ed. (New York: Free Press, 2008).

[2]Geert Hofstede and Gert Jan Hofstede, *Cultures and Organizations: Software of the Mind*, 2nd ed. (New York: McGraw-Hill, 2005).

[3]Fons Trompenaars and Charles Hampden-Turner, *Riding the Waves of Culture: Understanding Cultural Diversity in Business*, 2nd ed. (London: Nicholas Brealey, 1997).

[4]Robert J. House et al., eds., *Culture, Leadership and Organizations: The GLOBE Study of 62 Societies* (Thousand Oaks, Calif.: Sage, 2004).

[5]Ibid., p. xv.

[6]John W. Berry et al., *Crosscultural Psychology: Research and Applications* (New York: Cambridge University Press, 1992), p. 401.

[7]Harry C. Triandis, foreword to *Culture, Leadership and Organizations: The GLOBE Study of 62 Societies*, ed. Robert J. House et al. (Thousand Oaks, Calif.: Sage, 2004).

[8]House, *Culture, Leadership and Organizations*, p. 517.

[9]Hofstede and Hofstede, *Cultures and Organizations*, p. 46.

[10]Ibid., pp. 43-44.

[11]Dale Carl, Vipin Gupta and Mansour Javidan, "Power Distance," in *Culture, Leadership and Organizations*, ed. Robert J. House et al. (Thousand Oaks, Calif.: Sage, 2004), p. 539.

[12]Hofstede and Hofstede, *Cultures and Organizations*, p. 50.

[13]Carl, Gupta, Javidan, "Power Distance," p. 520.

[14]Ibid. p. 521.

[15]Ibid. p. 539.

[16]Hofstede and Hofstede, *Cultures and Organizations*, p. 43; Carl, Gupta and Javidan, "Power Distance," p. 539.

[17]Carl, Gupta, Javidan, "Power Distance," p. 523.

[18]Hofstede and Hofstede, *Cultures and Organizations*, p. 43.

[19]Carl, Gupta, Javidan, "Power Distance," p. 523.

[20]Hofstede and Hofstede, *Cultures and Organizations*, p. 43.

[21]A good discussion of the relationship between the history of China, power and Confucian values is in Edward J. Lazzerini and Richard Yang, "The World of China," in *The World of Asia*, ed. Akira Iriye, 2nd ed. (Wheeling, Ill.: Harlan Davidson, 1995); and also Lucian W. Pye and Mary W. Pye, *Asian Power and Politics: The Cultural Dimensions of Authority* (Cambridge, Mass.: Belknap, 1985).

[22]Carl, Gupta, Javidan, "Power Distance," p. 559.

[23]Evan Ramstad, "Pulling Rank Gets Harder at One Korean Company," *The Wall Street Journal*, August 20, 2007, p. B1.

[24]Carl, Gupta, Javidan, "Power Distance," p. 559. Several anthropologists would challenge the statement as culturally biased. See Richard A. Schweder, "Moral Maps, 'First World' Conceits, and the New Evangelists," in *Culture Matters: How Values Shape Human Progress*, ed. Lawrence E. Harrison and Samuel P. Huntington (New York: Basic Books, 2000).

[25]Hofstede and Hofstede, *Cultures and Organizations*, p. 62; and House, *Culture, Leadership and Organizations*, p. 558. See the corruption index by Transparency International at <http://www.transparency.org>.

[26]Carl, Gupta, Javidan, "Power Distance," pp. 557-58.

[27]For further information on the debate see Glen J. Schwartz, "It's Time to Get Serious About the Cycle of Dependency in Africa," *Evangelical Missions Quarterly,* April 1993, pp. 126-30. On the other side Bob Finley argues that the only way to give toward missions is by supporting nationals. Bob Finley, *Reformation in Foreign Missions* (Longwood, Fla.: Xulon, 2005). For an article that seeks to find a middle way, see James E. Plueddemann, "Beyond Independence to Mature Partnership," *Evangelical Missions Quarterly* 19, no. 1 (January 1983): 48-55; and Byang H. Kato, "Aid to the National Church: When It Helps, When It Hinders," *Evangelical Missions Quarterly,* Summer 1972, pp. 193-201.

[28]For a good discussion on multicultural teams, see Lianne Roembke, *Building Credible Multicultural Teams* (Pasadena, Calif.: William Carey Library, 2000).

[29]Marvin K. Mayers, *Christianity Confronts Culture* (Grand Rapids: Zondervan, 1974), pp. 149-54. The concepts have been expanded in Sherwood G. Lingenfelter and Marvin K. Mayers, *Ministering Crossculturally* (Grand Rapids: Baker, 1986).

[30]This excerpt is taken from "The Christian Vision Project: The African Planter" (an interview with Oscar Muriu, posted April 1, 2007), pp. 6-7, *Leadershipjournal.net* <http://www.christianitytoday.com/le/2007/002/3.96.html>. Used by permission.

### Chapter 7: Leadership and Individualism

[1]Fons Trompenaars and Charles Hampden-Turner, *Riding the Waves of Culture: Understanding Cultural Diversity in Business,* 2nd ed. (London: Nicholas Brealey, 1997), p. 58.

[2]Ibid.

[3]Duane Elmer, *Cross-Cultural Connections* (Downers Grove, Ill.: InterVarsity Press, 2002), p. 134.

[4]Robert J. House et al., eds., *Culture, Leadership and Organizations: The GLOBE Study of 62 Societies* (Thousand Oaks, Calif.: Sage, 2004), p. 438.

[5]Trompenaars and Hamden-Turner, *Riding the Waves of Culture,* p. 50.

[6]Ibid., p. 54.

[7]Ibid., p. 55.

[8]Geert Hofstede and Gert Jan Hofstede, *Cultures and Organizations: Software of the Mind,* 2nd ed. (New York: McGraw-Hill, 2005), p. 74.

[9]Ibid., p. 75.

[10]Ibid.

[11]Ibid., pp. 78-79.

[12]Michele J. Gefand et al., "Individualism and Collectivism," in *Culture, Leadership and Organizations: The GLOBE Study of 62 Societies,* ed. Robert J. House et al. (Thousand Oaks, Calif.: Sage, 2004), pp. 464-65.

[13]According to the GLOBE study, the term *Anglo* includes Canada, the U.S.A., Australia, Ireland, England, White South Africa and New Zealand.

[14]Vipin Gupta, Paul Hanges, Peter Dorfman and Robert House, "Regional and Climate Clustering of Societal Cultures," in *Culture, Leadership and Organizations: The GLOBE Study of 62 Societies,* ed. Robert J. House et al. (Thousand Oaks, Calif.: Sage, 2004), pp. 193-94.

[15]Ibid., p. 194.

[16]Malcolm Gladwell, *Outliers: The Story of Success* (New York: Little, Brown, 2008), p. 166.

[17]Ibid., pp. 166-67.

[18]Ibid., p. 175.

[19]Ibid., p. 174.

[20]Hofstede and Hofstede, *Cultures and Organizations*, p. 82.

[21]Ibid., p. 89.

[22]Paul G. Hiebert, *Anthropological Insights for Missionaries* (Grand Rapids: Baker, 1985), p. 212.

[23]Ibid., p. 213.

[24]Ibid., p. 212.

[25]Hofstede and Hofstede, *Cultures and Organizations*, p. 99.

[26]Ibid., p. 100.

[27]Ibid., p. 102.

[28]Martin Luther King, Jr., "I Have a Dream," delivered August 28, 1963, at the Lincoln Memorial, Washington, D.C. Found at <http://www.americanrhetoric.com/speeches/mlkihaveadream.htm>.

Chapter 8: Leadership and Ambiguity

[1]Edward T. Hall, *Beyond Culture* (Garden City, N.Y.: Anchor, 1976), p. 41.

[2]Geert Hofstede and Gert Jan Hofstede, *Cultures and Organizations: Software of the Mind*, 2nd ed. (New York: McGraw-Hill, 2005), p. 167.

[3]Ibid., p. 173.

[4]Ibid., p. 176.

[5]Mary Sully de Luque and Mansour Javidan, "Uncertainty Avoidance," in *Culture, Leadership and Organizations*, ed. Robert J. House et al. (Thousand Oaks, Calif.: Sage, 2004), p. 602.

[6]Ibid., p. 603.

[7]Ibid., p. 618.

[8]Ibid.

[9]Ibid., p. 619 (both of these questions were reversed scored).

[10]Ibid., pp. 621-22.

[11]Ibid., pp. 636-37.

[12]Ibid., p. 624.

[13]Ibid., p. 621.

[14]Ibid., p. 631.

[15]Ibid., pp. 631-32.

[16]Ruth A. Tucker, *From Jerusalem to Irian Jaya: A Biographical History of Missions*, 2nd ed. (Grand Rapids: Zondervan, 2004), p. 192; also see Stephen Neill, *A History of Christian Missions* (New York: Penguin, 1964), p. 283.

[17]For further information consult the IMB website (copyright 2006–2009) <http://www.imb.org/main/page.asp?StoryID=4486&LanguageID=1709>.

[18]"The Foundational Values of Youth With A Mission," released February 2004, The Official YWAM International Website <http://www.ywam.org/contents/abo_doc_values.htm>.

[19]"YWAM's Structure," The Official YWAM International Website (copyright 2004) <http://www.ywam.org/contents/abo_wha_structure.htm>.

[20]Ori Brafman and Rod A. Beckstrom, *The Starfish and the Spider: The Unstoppable Power of Leaderless Organizations* (New York: Portfolio, 2006).

[21]Ibid., p. 35.

[22]Ibid., p. 19.

[23]Ibid., p. 20.

[24]Note the decentralization described in the YWAM website: "YWAM does not have an international administrative office that maintains a database of every YWAM staff and YWAM alumni. If you want to connect with a person in YWAM, please contact the location they work with directly or their last known location. Another avenue is to try other YWAM connect sites." "Questions About YWAM," The Official YWAM International Website (copyright 2004) <http://www.ywam.org/contents/abo_Commonquest.htm>.

[25]Charles Handy, *The Age of Paradox* (Boston: Harvard Business School Press, 1994).

[26]Ibid., p. 110.

[27]Ibid., p. 135.

[28]Ibid.

[29]For a detailed description of the growth of the Kale Heywat Church, see Raymond Davis, *Fire on the Mountain* (New York/Toronto: SIM, 1966); F. Peter Cotterell, *Born at Midnight* (Chicago: Moody Press, 1973).

[30]Samuel Escobar, *The New Global Mission: The Gospel from Everywhere to Everyone* (Downers Grove, Ill.: InterVarsity Press, 2003), see chap. 10, "A New Way of Looking at the World."

[31]Samuel Escobar, "Evangelical Missiology: Peering into the Future," in *Global Missiology for the 21st Century*, ed. William D. Taylor (Grand Rapids: Baker Academic, 2000), pp. 101-22.

[32]Ibid., p. 107.

[33]Ibid., p. 109.

[34]David Tai-Woong Lee, "A Two-Thirds World Evaluation of Contemporary Missiology," in *Global Missiology for the 21st Century*, ed. William D. Taylor (Grand Rapids: Baker Academic, 2000), p. 140.

[35]For a further discussion of my thoughts on goals, see my article "Measurable Objectives, No! Faith Goals, Yes!" *Evangelical Missions Quarterly* 31, no. 2 (April 1995): 184-87.

[36]Personal correspondence with Charlie Davis.

### Chapter 9: A Theology of Leadership

[1]Paul Hersey and Kenneth H. Blanchard, *Management of Organizational Behavior*, 5th ed. (Englewood Cliffs, N.J.: Prentice-Hall, 1969).

[2]The model is adapted from one used to analyze educational philosophy by William K. Frankena, *Philosophy of Education* (Toronto: Macmillan, 1965), pp. 4-10.

[3]The quote is attributed to Lord Acton (1834-1902) in a letter to Bishop Mandell Creighton in 1887 <http://www.phrases.org.uk/meanings/288200.html>.

[4]See Dinesh D'Souza, *What's So Great About Christianity* (Washington, D.C.: Regnery, 2007). He writes, "Christianity enhanced the notion of political and social accountability by providing a new model: that of servant leadership. In ancient Greece and Rome no one would have dreamed of considering political leaders anyone's servants. The job of the leader was to lead" (p. 81).

Chapter 10: A Theory of Leadership

[1]See "Edwin E. Plueddemann—Hall of Fame Entry," (written in 1988, posted March 29, 2004) on The Plastics Academy's Hall of Fame website <http://www .plasticshalloffame.com/articles.php?articleId=106>.
[2]K. L. Mittal, ed., *Silane and Other Coupling Agents: Festschrift in Honor of the 75th Birthday of Dr. Edwin P. Plueddemann* (The Netherlands: VSP BV, 1992), see pp. xi-xiv.
[3]The Greek word for leadership in Rom 12:8 is *proistēmi*, which can mean "to set over," "be a protector," "give aid" or "manage."
[4]For some people the crucial issue regarding women in leadership has to do with ordination of women. Because several of my ideas are rather iconoclastic, I put them in the footnotes. One of my controversial positions is that I don't believe that "ordination" is a New Testament concept. A major difference between the Old and New Testaments is the New Testament "priesthood of all believers." After the Old Testament, priesthood was discontinued and now the Holy Spirit equally fills both men and women, so there now is no need for the Old Testament institution of ordination. I don't "pound the pulpit" on this idea.
[5]Some say that Paul told Timothy that women in the church in Ephesus should not teach in the church because women are more prone to heresy. But such thinking leads to illogical conclusions. If women are more prone to be false teachers, they should never be allowed to teach women or children. Men should not sing hymns written by women, and women should not be allowed to write books. This is silly. After all, most of the heretics in the Bible were men.
[6]Also see Jim and Carol Plueddemann, *Pilgrims in Progress* (Wheaton, Ill.: Harold Shaw, 1990), pp. 72-73.
[7]Taken from "National Leader of the Month for November 2007: C. William Pollard," on the LeaderNetwork.org website <http://www.leadernetwork.org/william_ pollard_november_07.htm/>.
[8]Wes Roberts, *Leadership Secrets of Attila the Hun* (New York: Warner Books, 1985); Robert D. Kaplan, *Warrior Politics: Why Leadership Demands a Pagan Ethos* (New York: Vintage, 2002); Steven B. Sample, *The Contrarian's Guide to Leadership* (San Francisco: Jossey-Bass, 2002).
[9]Jack Welch with John A. Byrne, *Jack, Straight from the Gut* (New York: Warner Books, 2001); see the chapter called "The People Factory," pp. 154-68.
[10]There are many good leadership books written for the secular audience. I have learned much from the writings of Charles Handy, Stephen R. Covey, Jim Collins and many others.
[11]Charles Handy, *The Gods of Management* (New York: Oxford University Press, 1978).
[12]Fons Trompenaars and Charles Hampden-Turner, *Riding the Waves of Culture: Understanding Cultural Diversity in Business*, 2nd ed. (London: Nicholas Brealey, 1997), pp. 157-78.
[13]Ibid., p. 175.
[14]Robert J. House et al., eds., *Culture, Leadership and Organizations: The GLOBE Study of 62 Societies* (Thousand Oaks, Calif.: Sage, 2004), pp. 6-7.
[15]See the chapter on pilgrim leaders in the book by Jim and Carol Plueddemann, *Pilgrims in Progress* (Wheaton, Ill.: Harold Shaw, 1990), pp. 63-76.

## Chapter 11: Developing Vision and Strategy

[1]James E. Plueddemann, "Measurable Objectives, No! Faith Goals, Yes!" *Evangelical Missions Quarterly* 31, no. 2 (April 1995): 184-87. (This article received so many letters to the editor that the editor published them in the next two editions. Most of the comments were negative and reflected a low-context worldview.)

[2]For another discussion of the metaphor see James E. Plueddemann, "Visionary Planning for World Missions," in *With an Eye on the Future: Development and Mission in the 21st Century; Essays in Honor of Ted Ward*, ed. Duane Elmer and Lois McKinney (Monrovia, Calif.: MARC, 1996).

[3]See Jim Plueddemann, "SIM's Agenda for a Gracious Revolution," *International Bulletin of Missionary Research* (October 1999): 156-60.

[4]Peter Drucker, *The Effective Executive* (London: Pan, 1967), p. 151.

[5]From a confidential prayer letter.

[6]Tabitha Plueddemann, personal correspondence.

## Chapter 12: Developing Global Leaders

[1]Robert Banks, *Reenvisioning Theological Education: Exploring a Missional Alternative to Current Models* (Grand Rapids: Eerdmans, 1999), p. 224.

[2]He cites research from Robert W. Ferris, *The Emphasis on Leadership as Servanthood* (Ann Arbor, Mich.: University Microfilms International, 1982), p. 159.

[3]Ted Ward, "Servants, Leaders, and Tyrants," in *With an Eye on the Future: Development and Mission in the 21st Century; Essays in Honor of Ted Ward*, ed. Duane Elmer and Lois McKinney (Monrovia, Calif.: MARC, 1996), pp. 29-30.

[4]Ibid., p. 36.

[5]Michael H. Hoppe, "Crosscultural Issues in Leadership Development," in *The Center for Creative Leadership Handbook of Leadership Development*, ed. Cynthia D. McCaulley, Russ S. Moxley and Ellen Van Velsor (San Francisco: Jossey Bass, 1998), pp. 340-41.

[6]Ibid., p. 341.

[7]M. G. Smith, "The Hausa of Northern Nigeria," in *Peoples of Africa*, ed. James L. Gibbs Jr. (Chicago: Holt, Rinehart & Winston, 1965), pp. 135, 139.

[8]Phoebe Ottenberg, "The Afikpo Ibo of Eastern Nigeria," in *Peoples of Africa*, ed. James L. Gibbs Jr. (Chicago: Holt, Rinehart & Winston, 1965), p. 19.

[9]P. C. Lloyd, "The Yoruba of Nigeria," in *Peoples of Africa*, ed. James L. Gibbs Jr. (Chicago: Holt, Rinehart & Winston, 1965), p. 568.

[10]James E. Plueddemann, "The Power of Piaget," in *Nurture That Is Christian*, ed. James C. Wilhoit and John M. Dettoni (Wheaton, Ill.: Victor Books, 1995), p. 51. See Barry J. Wadsworth, *Piaget's Theory of Cognitive Development* (New York: David McKay, 1971).

[11]Horace Bushnell, *Christian Nurture* (New York: Scribner, 1861). p. 10.

[12]This concept is common to most developmental theorists. The term "disorienting dilemmas" is used by Jack Mezirow, *Transformative Dimensions of Adult Learning* (San Francisco: Jossey Bass, 1991), p. 197.

[13]Jack Weatherford, *Genghis Khan and the Making of the Modern World* (New York: Three Rivers, 2004), p. xviii.

[14]Ibid., p. 53.

[15]Ibid., p. 76.

[16]Ibid., p. xviii.
[17]These suggestions come from personal experience and from valuable insights from C. Brooklyn Derr, Sylvie Roussillon and Frank Bournois, eds., *Crosscultural Approaches to Leadership Development* (Westport, Conn.: Quorum, 2001).

## Epilogue

[1]"Can We Work Together?" *Serving in Mission Together,* issue 119, Fall 2007, p. 3.
[2]Philip R. Harris, Robert T. Moran and Sarah V. Moran, *Managing Cultural Differences: Global Leadership Strategies for the Twenty-First Century,* 6th ed. (New York: Elsevier Butterworth-Heinemann, 2004), p. 25.
[3]Howard Brant, personal correspondence.

# RECOMMENDED READING

Bass, Bernard M., with Ruth Bass. *The Bass Handbook of Leadership: Theory, Research, and Management.* 4th ed. New York: Free Press, 2008.

Brafman, Ori, and Rod A. Beckstrom. *The Starfish and the Spider: The Unstoppable Power of Leaderless Organizations.* New York: Portfolio, 2006.

Elmer, Duane. *Cross-Cultural Conflict.* Downers Grove, Ill.: InterVarsity Press, 1993.

———. *Cross-Cultural Servanthood.* Downers Grove, Ill.: InterVarsity Press, 2006.

Escobar, Samuel. *The New Global Mission: The Gospel from Everywhere to Everyone.* Downers Grove, Ill.: InterVarsity Press, 2003.

Gladwell, Malcolm. *Outliers: The Story of Success.* New York: Little, Brown, 2008.

Hall, Edward T. *Beyond Culture.* Garden City, N.Y.: Anchor Press, 1976.

Hofstede, Geert, and Gert Jan Hofstede. *Cultures and Organizations: Software of the Mind.* 2nd ed. New York: McGraw-Hill, 2005.

House, Robert J., Paul J. Hanges, Mansour Javidan, Peter W. Dorfman and Vipin Gupta, eds. *Culture, Leadership and Organizations: The GLOBE Study of 62 Societies.* Thousand Oaks, Calif.: Sage, 2004.

Laniak, Timothy S. *While Shepherds Watched Their Flocks: Reflections on Biblical Leadership.* Charlotte, N.C.: Shepherd Leader Publishers, 2007 <www.shepherdleader.com>.

Lingenfelter, Sherwood G. *Leading Cross-Culturally: Covenant Relationships for Effective Christian Leadership.* Grand Rapids: Baker Academic, 2008.

Plueddemann, James E. "Theological Implications of Globalizing Missions." In *Globalizing Theology: Belief and Practice in an Era of World Christianity*, edited by Craig Ott and Harold A. Netland, pp. 250-66. Grand Rapids: Baker Academic, 2006.

Trompenaars, Fons, and Charles Hampden-Turner. *Riding the Waves of Culture: Understanding Cultural Diversity in Business*. 2nd ed. London: Nicholas Brealey, 1997.

# Index